One of the Dangerous Trades

**Poets on Poetry    Donald Hall, General Editor**

| | |
|---|---|
| DONALD HALL | *Goatfoot Milktongue Twinbird* |
| GALWAY KINNELL | *Walking Down the Stairs* |
| WILLIAM STAFFORD | *Writing the Australian Crawl* |
| DONALD DAVIE | *Trying to Explain* |
| MAXINE KUMIN | *To Make a Prairie* |
| DIANE WAKOSKI | *Toward a New Poetry* |
| ROBERT BLY | *Talking All Morning* |
| ROBERT FRANCIS | *Pot Shots at Poetry* |
| RICHARD KOSTELANETZ | *The Old Poetries and the New* |
| LOUIS SIMPSON | *A Company of Poets* |
| PHILIP LEVINE | *Don't Ask* |
| JOHN HAINES | *Living Off the Country* |
| MARGE PIERCY | *Parti-Colored Blocks for a Quilt* |
| DONALD HALL | *The Weather for Poetry* |
| JAMES WRIGHT | *Collected Prose* |
| MARVIN BELL | *Old Snow Just Melting* |
| ALICIA OSTRIKER | *Writing Like a Woman* |
| JOHN LOGAN | *A Ballet for the Ear* |
| HAYDEN CARRUTH | *Effluences from the Sacred Caves* |
| ROBERT HAYDEN | *Collected Prose* |
| DONALD JUSTICE | *Platonic Scripts* |
| JOHN FREDERICK NIMS | *A Local Habitation* |
| ANNE SEXTON | *No Evil Star* |
| CHARLES SIMIC | *The Uncertain Certainty* |
| LOUIS SIMPSON | *The Character of the Poet* |
| WILLIAM STAFFORD | *You Must Revise Your Life* |
| TESS GALLAGHER | *A Concert of Tenses* |
| WELDON KEES | *Reviews and Essays, 1936–55* |
| DONALD HALL | *Poetry and Ambition* |
| CHARLES WRIGHT | *Halflife* |
| WILLIAM MATTHEWS | *Curiosities* |
| CHARLES SIMIC | *Wonderful Words, Silent Truth* |
| TOM CLARK | *The Poetry Beat* |
| WILLIAM MEREDITH | *Poems Are Hard to Read* |
| PETER DAVISON | *One of the Dangerous Trades* |

*Peter Davison*

# One of the
# Dangerous Trades

ESSAYS ON THE
WORK AND WORKINGS
OF POETRY

Ann Arbor
The University of Michigan Press

Copyright © by the University of Michigan 1991
All rights reserved
Published in the United States of America by
The University of Michigan Press
Manufactured in the United States of America

1994   1993   1992   1991   4   3   2   1

**Library of Congress Cataloging-in-Publication Data**

Davison, Peter.
    One of the dangerous trades : essays on the work and workings of
poetry / Peter Davison.
        p.     cm. — (Poets on poetry)
    Includes bibliographical references.
    ISBN 0-472-09407-6 (cloth : alk.). — ISBN 0-472-06407-X (paper :
alk.)
    1. American poetry—20th century—History and criticism.
    2. English poetry—History and criticism.   3. Poetry.     I. Title.
II. Series.
PS323.5.D38   1991
811.009—dc20                                                        90-28570
                                                                              CIP

**British Library Cataloguing in Publication Data**

Davison, Peter
    One of the dangerous trades : essays on the work and
    workings of poetry.
    1. Poetry—critical studies
    I. Title
    809.1

    ISBN 0-472-09407-6

Distributed in the United Kingdom and Europe by
Manchester University Press, Oxford Road,
Manchester M13 9PL, UK

Dedicated to *The Atlantic Monthly*,
in memory of its friends, and mine

Charles W. Morton
Edwin O'Connor
Arthur H. Thornhill
Donald B. Snyder
Edward Weeks
Louise Desaulniers

# Acknowledgments

*Grateful acknowledgment is made to the following journals and publishers for permission to reprint previously published material.*

*The Atlantic Monthly* for "The Perils of Reputation," "The Great Grassy World from Both Sides," "Sylvia Plath: *Ariel*," "Sylvia Plath: *Crossing the Water*," "A New Generation," "Space, Time, and Silence," and "Visionaries."

Northeastern University Press for "Lucia Maria Perillo," from *Dangerous Life* by Lucia Maria Perillo. Copyright © 1989 by Lucia Maria Perillo. Reprinted with the permission of Northeastern University Press.

*The Writer* for "Poems Happen," which originally appeared under the title "Time and the Poet."

*Every effort has been made to trace the ownership of all copyrighted material in this book and to obtain permission for its use.*

# Preface: From a Poetry Editor

During most of my writing life I have felt slightly estranged from my fellow poets. My friends and loved ones, of course, shift uneasily when I mention poetry in common conversation, but most poets seem to look at me sidewise, preferring me, I imagine, in the role of editor, for as editor I can remain that most desirable of beings, a means to an end. I once asked a poet and friend I intensely admired whether he might want to take a look at some of my unpublished poems, and he replied, in effect, why? He couldn't print them.

I have spent forty years as an editor, reading other people's manuscripts, encouraging other people's muses, discouraging those—both prose and poetry—that seemed to me unsuited to a partnership between us, helping bring texts into publishable condition, attempting to make the delicate compromise between publishing books of some degree of excellence and books sufficiently profitable to keep me employed and to keep their authors published. Editing came to me before poetry did, by a few years, yet I was raised in an atmosphere that positively reeked of poetry, a fragrance as strong as that of my father's cigars. I have never been able, despite years of interior struggle, fully to separate the processes of editing and poetry, though the conduct of each craft differs profoundly from the other and emerges from entirely different regions of the soul. Yet, such are the perils of appearances, I have by and large been seen as a poet by editors and as an editor by poets. I once playfully dictated my epitaph: "He was a better

*American Poetry Review* (March–April, 1991).

editor than other poets and a better poet than other editors."
I wonder unmercifully if it may not do me justice.

On a platform, reading poems to an audience, a poet is
attuned to seduce, or even command, attention to the signifi-
cance of his life and work; but if he makes such demands on
the listener's attention in common conversation, he will be
regarded as, at worst, rude; at best, egotistical. When poets sit
down together they tend to diminish their conversation to
shoptalk, gossip about poets, publication, and questions of the
poet's trade.

An editor has colleagues—other editors—but his daily visi-
tors, writers, wear the faces of suitors, malcontents, aspirants,
even sycophants. Do other poets have colleagues? I do not
seem to have been able to keep any. I have had no teachers,
only masters: Frost, Kunitz, Robert Penn Warren, Alfred
Kazin, Dudley Fitts, my father Edward Davison—but, to my
sorrow, few poets whom I could talk to as companions in the
art: for a brief while, Sylvia Plath, for a few years, L. E.
Sissman, at one time William Meredith, at another, Alastair
Reid. At times some of my assistant editors, all themselves
poets, but younger, at *The Atlantic Monthly*—Mary Jo Salter,
Linda Gregerson, Steven Cramer—shared a special relation-
ship, curiously more collegial than with other poets of my own
age, because they too, part of the time, were editors. I have
wondered how it would feel to share a venue with other poets,
a campus for example, nowadays the commonest refuge. I
know that some other poets do have colleagues and treat them
as such, showing them work in progress for reciprocal appre-
ciation and critique. But when I read the lives of the poets I
find that they for the most part have been as isolated as I. The
great poetic friendships—Wordsworth and Coleridge, Robert
Frost and Edward Thomas, Theodore Roethke and Stanley
Kunitz—have ranged from the temporary to the uneasy.

At an early age and for what seemed to me good reasons I
chose to avoid academic life and have never done more than
dip into it since I was twenty. This has, in the last forty years,
increasingly distanced me from the trade routes of other po-
ets who spend most of their time there; and it also has made
me ill-read and ignorant in some fields, especially contempo-

rary literary criticism. But university life has no monopoly on intellectual curiosity, and as an editor I have had the luck to edit books that have drawn me into passionate involvements with molecular biology, architecture, politics, anthropology, ethology, biography, psychiatry, history, and a dozen other subjects, including, of course, the arts of poetry and fiction. This editorial work has produced in my own poetry an enlargement of means, if not a sharpening of concentration.

Concentration, however, has proved problematical. Saul Bellow once spoke eloquently of Distraction and Attention as representing the polarities of our time. We are distracted by the diurnal, yet we avoid, at our peril, giving it too little of our attention; we summon attention to our lives, our work, our souls, and allow ourselves, at our peril, to be too deeply attentive. We are indeed divided, but why not? Nobody since childhood promised us life would not be dangerous.

Deciding in favor of editorial work produced some effects I could not have predicted. The roomful of students, watching all term long, knows the professor of writing better than the professor knows any of the students, but the editor knows the author better than the author knows the editor; occasionally better, the editor suspects, than the author knows himself. Few authors, from the editor's purview, think often of the editor as a person at all, merely a maternal source of nurture, money, and support. It's the editor's task, in fact, to encourage this sort of transference, to help dispel the author's tunnel vision by becoming the most sympathetic and supportive, yet most discriminating, of readers, and undergoing a sort of counter-transference. In truth the editor depends no less— speaking of money—on the author's productivity than the teacher or psychoanalyst depends on the student's tuition or the patient's fees. The writer feels it differently, feels dependent on the editor and on the publisher's treasury, but an editor without writers is an editor without a living.

In fact, however, they depend on one another. I dare not inquire whether I chose to be an editor for the sake of that interdependence: to maintain a sort of guarded control where other writers were concerned. I dare not even speculate whether playing the role of editor gave me an excuse to vacate at will the more vulnerable identity of poet, to take shelter in the lee of an outwardly directed responsibility. Editing, however, also exposed me to the most explicit form of competition: sponsoring and advocating books as commodities in the marketplace where books jostle for the public's attention.

No one would claim that the academy lacks the competitive impulse! Academic forms of competition, however, require skills that resemble those of the courtier. Though in some ways editing resembles teaching, there is no way it resembles scholarship. There is little about editing that corresponds to the scholar's saraband with the learned world, the professional association, the department, the academic senate, the provost. Academic life calls for modes of behavior and negotiation that differ profoundly from those the editor uses to deal with the author, the agent, the art director, the publicist, the sales department, the president of the corporation, the board of directors, and, occasionally, the stockholders. Editors report to some managerial hierarch; professors have, or desire, tenure without limit of time, after which they report only to the consensus of their peers. The editor knows nothing of tenure: his success, like the poet's, must be proven every time he ventures onto paper, into print, or shifts allegiance as hireling from one publishing institution to another.

Even more significantly, poetry *qua* poetry knows little of hierarchy, nothing of tenure. Yes, that poet is better than I am, more gifted, more assured, more possessed of art or scope. But our relation to our work is the same. Poetry is in this sense the realm of the eternal amateur, which is why highly professionalized people distrust it. They do not share the feelings of being overcome, the shaking of the knees, the pounding of the heart.

In the world of publishing, economic competition ultimately prevails; in the world of poetry, the good opinion of fellow poets stands up as the highest short-term reward, as public acceptance will in the long term. Critical acceptance is fickle: it comes and goes. In the world where poets are employed as teachers, however, yet another form of ranking has gradually taken over: accreditation. What has the introduction of teaching into poetry done to alter the poetry Americans write? What if anything was changed when poetry began to be accredited by professors of writing, taking over from professors of English, who, earlier in this century, had taken their turn at accrediting what had previously been mere literature?

Poetry in advanced civilizations has always failed, despite its solitary aspirations, to avoid entanglement with institutions—at least, it has failed in such avoidance the more ambitious it became. Aeschylus seemed to speak for the Athenian Republic; Virgil for the Imperium of Augustus; Dante for the Holy Roman Empire; Shakespeare for the swashbuckling monarchy of Elizabeth I; Tennyson for the emotionally repressive but powerfully sentimental monarchy of Victoria; Whitman for the eloquently democratic presidency of Lincoln; Claudel for transmontane Catholicism, and so on. Sappho, Emily Dickinson, George Herbert, William Blake, Anna Akhmatova escaped such involvement. John Clare was institutionalized in one way, Gerard Manley Hopkins in another.

For what institution should poetry speak in an age when all institutions do inform against it? The great modernist writers of the West are notorious for having been mostly elitists, mostly antidemocratic. In the Soviet Union poetry flourished, in the work of Akhmatova and Mandelstam, despite the implacable fist of Stalinist tyranny. In Britain poetry lost much of its zest during the egalitarian postwar suzerainty of the Labour party but somehow recovered under the predatory individualist Margaret Thatcher. American poetry exclaimed against our involvement in the Vietnam War—feebly and forgettably for the most part—but flowered over the next two decades, in the work of women, especially as they successfully dismantled many fortified institutions. Other special subspecies of *Poeta Americana* allied themselves with special institutions, as for example those who took up the hieratic procedures of art journalism as a trade, in preference to the creative writing programs. Some other poets seemed to be willing to pay any social price to keep out of the universities: silence, exile, cunning. Reykjavik, Alaska, Hawaii.

Patience, more than anything else, ensures bloom in poetry. Those who rush at the Muse may well frighten her away; but poets like Stanley Kunitz, steadily laboring to create three or four poems a year for six decades, are more likely to win the Muse than many who woo more abruptly. Who would rather have written all the hundreds of poems too precipitately printed by Robert Lowell than the mere scores of poems of Elizabeth Bishop, or even those few poems Emily Dickinson published in her lifetime? Too many poets have too often hustled poems into print that would have been better left asleep. The point is to be able, by habit, by luck, and by contriving a fecund way of life, to find one's way back to Concentration, the concentration the poet simply has to be able to call upon—not necessarily at will, but at times. Nothing else, no matter what disguises we adopt or how we choose to make a living, characterizes the poet as an artist more exquisitely than this verbally meticulous, sensuously specific, image-borne, music-induced variety of concentration, for other artists are by comparison specialized and abstract. To lose concentration is the poet's principal peril; to concentrate too hard and long, as Plath and Berryman and Schwartz and other extremists did, is to risk Distraction, distraction sufficient to claim one's very life. There are various trades one can choose, but—as with Judaism—no one can choose the vocation of poetry. For that you are chosen, and your destiny then offers you a great many tradeoffs, all of them dangerous:

Obscurity vs. Banality
Pomposity vs. False Modesty
Cowardice vs. Bravado
Cronyism vs. Isolation
Insanity vs. Conformity
Sale of Talent vs. Invisibility
Talent Ruined by Anxiety vs. Talent Ruined by Neglect
And, finally, Distraction vs. Attention.

If you choose obscurity, you may find it. If you choose to be a mover and shaker in the tiny world of poetic influence, you may lose all the poetry that has been given you, while gaining influence over . . . what? If you choose to give yourself over entirely to your students, they are likely to take you up on the offer. If you choose to set up as an authority on poetry, you may succeed, while losing the humility that enables you to write it. If you declare yourself a "professional," you may lose your amateur status, without which no poet survives. If you set yourself up as a poetic entrepreneur, you will most likely find that, literally and figuratively, poetry is an imaginary business, with no market for the product. No wonder that, though every sensitive person feels like a poet, if only for a few short nights or weeks in his or her teens, the muse most often deserts: "They flee from me that sometime did me seek. . . ."

There is no safety in poetry, least of all safety in numbers, regardless of how many more poets we see writing their work, and how many—or few—readers reading it. Poetry cannot help making a connection between a poet and others, sometimes when they are alone with it in a room, reading; sometimes when they are together with it in a room, listening. Poetry brings us together, it allies us in the knowledge of loneliness, of joy, of loss, of pain, of tenderness. We should all memorize a store of poetry in case someone decides for any reason to haul us into solitary confinement, especially since, in this century as in others, a deep dedication to poetry has a very good chance of landing us there.

This book is made up of my reflections on the work of contemporary poetry, the work of poets, the work of being a poet, and the dangers such work exposes us to—*us* meaning poets, *us* meaning readers. But the poet, whether the name be Akhmatova or Frost, Neruda or Montale, Trakl or Larkin, has to make a trade; the reader need only turn his back. I have felt it proper, with two exceptions, to omit from this volume the praises of living poets whose work I have sponsored for publication. Therefore I have omitted from this thirty-year show my views on poets I have admired deeply enough to publish: Mary Oliver, David Ignatow, David Wagoner, John Malcolm Brinnin, Donald Hall, William Matthews, Thomas Lux, Rodney Jones, Andrew Hudgins, James Tate, Margaret Atwood, George Starbuck, and others. Some of the poets I do speak of are or were friends, some dear friends; others I have never or hardly met. But, for reasons that may lie entirely at my door, though some of these poets have been my masters, none has, exactly, been my colleague. Collegiality in poetry may, it turns out, be limited to colleges: yet even on campuses one hears complaints.

That is one of the most dangerous things about the trade. To the extent that we give ourselves to poetry we give up the safety of trades, we deny ourselves economic value in order to claim a value of another, and, we believe, higher, kind. That may be the most dangerous claim of all, for to give yourself to poetry you have to bet your life on it, as Frost used to say. He, in turn, in his most profound poem, "Directive," referred us to St. Mark, who quotes Jesus as saying, again and again, "He that hath ears to hear, let him hear," and then "Whosoever will save his life shall lose it. . . ."

Not a dangerous trade? The hell you say.

Gloucester, Massachusetts
June 17, 1990

# Contents

I. PERILS

One of the Dangerous Trades      3

The Great Predicament of Poetry      11

The Refuge of the Present Tense      17

The Perils of Reputation      20

In Quest to Have Extreme      27

The Great Grassy World from Both Sides:
The Poetry of Robert Lowell and James
Dickey at Mid-Career      37

II. ADMIRATIONS

The Last Word: In Remembrance of
Alexander Pope      57

"Quit Ye Like Men": The Maturing of
Robert Frost      63

Robert Frost: "I Want People to Understand
Me—But I Want Them to Understand Me
Wrong."      79

Sylvia Plath 1: *Ariel*      84

Sylvia Plath 2: *Crossing the Water*      88

Sylvia Plath 3: *Letters Home*      93

Sylvia Plath 4: *The Journals*      95

Sylvia Plath 5: *Ariel Ascending*                                    99

Wallace Stevens                                                     101

"Deep in the Blackness of Woods": A
    Farewell to Robert Penn Warren                           105

Stanley Kunitz at Eighty                                           113

The Sandpiper Poetry of Elizabeth Bishop                           117

The Saddest Englishman: Philip Larkin                              123

III. CONTEMPORARIES

A New Generation                                                   131

L. E. Sissman: "Did Shriner Die or Make It
    to New York?"                                            139

Space, Time, and Silence: Merwin, Strand,
    and Ammons                                                148

Visionaries: Kinnell and Wright                                    155

Poets of Exile and Isolation: Walcott, Koch,
    Simic, and Carruth                                        161

The Sanity of *Human Wishes:* Robert Hass                          167

Lucia Maria Perillo: *Dangerous Life*                              172

IV. SELF-APPRAISAL

Poems Happen                                                       177

Praying Wrong: An Interview                                        180

Self-Portrait: Sources, Impacts, Decisions                         192

*His bills of lading were rhymed no matter how he tried to avoid it, and routine business letters had a lyrical spirit that diminished their authority. . . . He fulfilled all his duties with admirable skill, studying every thread in that mysterious warp that had so much to do with the offices of poetry, but he never won the honor he most desired, which was to write one, just one, acceptable business letter. Without intending to, without even knowing it, he demonstrated with his life that his father had been right when he repeated until his dying day that there was no one with more common sense, no stonecutter more obstinate, no manager more lucid or dangerous, than a poet.*

— Gabriel García Márquez,
*Love in the Time of Cholera,*
translated by Edith Grossman

# I

# Perils

# One of the Dangerous Trades

If poetry has "lost its audience," if we have undergone a "vast cultural change" [the thesis for the symposium to which this paper was contributed], might it not be as valid to assess the changes in society as to belabor the oft-lamented tendencies in our poetry? Professor Christopher Clausen's challenge for contemporary poets delivers the familiar impact of a slap on the wrist. He, like everyone, asks why we are not read by everyone, as poets were in the golden age, as Mao Tse-tung and Yevtushenko and Rod McKuen are. Whatever are poets doing wrong? Why do poets "conspire" to "create an impression" that "the need for poetry is less in our era" than formerly? Osip Mandelstam answered us with dreadful irony from the Soviet side: "Why do you complain? Poetry is respected only in this country—people are killed for it. There's no place where more people are killed for it."[1]

No one would claim that our poets are doing everything right. There are too many of us writing and not enough of us reading, and all of us are talking to ourselves. But such phenomena as the Poets-in-the-Schools program, and other trends in education, to say nothing of a generalized suspicion of traditional academic training, have all created in the last thirty-five years a revolution of entitlement where poetry (and many other arts) are concerned. Everyone has the right to be trained as a poet, if training, indeed, is the right word. We have devel-

---

*The Georgia Review* (Winter 1981).
[1]Osip Mandelstam, quoted in *Hope Against Hope: A Memoir,* by Nadezhda Mandelstam, trans. Max Hayward (New York: Atheneum Publishers, 1970), p. 159.

oped an entire educational system of poet-think, of schools and graduate schools, and workshops, and conferences, and residencies, where bards link up like chains of algae, funded by state councils and federal grants and half-suspecting taxpayers. It seems odd how seldom anyone points out that the prime force affecting the state of poetry in the United States today is the State. It also seems odd that almost no one thinks of this as holding any hint of danger for poetry. Far from it: the moment we hear a threat of reduction in federal spending for the arts, art-advocates take to the streets.

The truth is, there is scarcely a poet practicing today who has not been rewarded, in some degree, by the government for the teaching of his craft or for reading her work in public or for appearing in the schools—or even, in rare cases, for actually writing poems. I believe this to be unprecedented in history—though Robert Hass, who knows everything, once told me that poets were similarly supported in the Sung Dynasty, if I remember rightly, as appendages of the court.

Everywhere we hear the old cry revived that poets are not noble enough (or not "democratic" enough, meaning ignoble enough?) for these times. I beg to suggest that this cry sounds hollow. Mr. Clausen's view at any rate rests on simplism. For one thing, his citations mislead. Frost, for example, never defined poetry so crudely as to call it "a clarification of life," though Clausen says so. Frost in actuality entered a demur more interesting than the plea: "It begins in delight, it inclines to the impulse, it assumes direction with the first line laid down, it runs a course of lucky events, and ends in a clarification of life—not necessarily a great clarification, such as sects and cults are founded on, but a momentary stay against confusion. It has denouement." This hardly resembles what Clausen says Frost says. The poem *ends* in a clarification of life, but that is not the figure a poem makes. "The figure," Frost says at the outset, "is the same as for love."[2]

When Clausen turns to Williams, we find him quoting the slogan "No ideas but in things." But the opening of *Paterson*,

---

[2]Robert Frost, "The Figure a Poem Makes," from *Complete Poems of Robert Frost* (New York: Henry Holt and Company, 1949), p. vi.

like the introduction to Frost's 1949 *Complete Poems,* which I have just quoted, operates far more conditionally and allusively than a hornbook maxim: "a confession," Williams writes, "a basket; a column; a reply to Greek and Latin with the bare hands; a gathering up; a celebration; / in distinctive terms; by multiplication a reduction to one; daring; a fall; the clouds resolved into a sandy sluice; an enforced pause." It isn't till several pages later, in the body of the poem, that Williams arrives at the slogan, and then he immediately qualifies it:

> —Say it, no ideas but in things—
> nothing but the blank faces of the houses
> and cylindrical trees
> bent, forked by preconception and accident . . .[3]

That last line of Williams's might even describe the position of poetry now, forked as it is between our preconceptions of poetry's role and the accidents that it has undergone. We have been taught—and were we wrongly taught?—that good poetry should be memorable. Yet who can remember the lines we read in the magazines? Stanley Kunitz, with characteristic depth and irony, has written that poetry today is easier to write but harder to remember than formerly—a remark that reflects as cuttingly upon us as readers as it does upon writers.

Then there is the fork of accident, the sort of accident in which an infant is suffocated. Unlike the Russians, we do not kill poets except with kindness—an indication, perhaps, of the degree of seriousness we entertain. We fund their fellowships, we smile at their outcries, their craziness, we work up glamor from their suicides and blame it all on poetry—although, as I have written elsewhere, we must

> Admit
> that poetry is one of the dangerous trades.
> No matter how many we know who have been goaded
> by its black promises to deliver

---

[3]William Carlos Williams, *Paterson* (New York: New Directions, 1963), pp. 10, 14.

> their bodies to the blue snowdrift of death,
> it was not poetry, but life, they died of.
>
> ("The Obituary Writer")[4]

Ted Hughes, introducing Sylvia Plath's stories, *Johnny Panic and the Bible of Dreams,* wrote about his wife's ambitions during the early 1960s: "Successful story-writing, for her, had all the advantages of a top job. She wanted the cash, and the freedom that can go with it. She wanted the professional standing, as a big earner, as the master of a difficult trade, and as a serious investigator into the real world. . . . Her dogged, year-in year-out effort to write conventional fiction, in the hope of preparing herself to make a livelihood, was like a persistent refusal of her genius."[5] In those days the road to success looked clear: a *Mademoiselle* Guest Editorship, followed by a first-reading contract with the *New Yorker.* Today the poet aches for an NEA Fellowship, a tenured Creative Writing position, and summer stints at Bread Loaf or Yaddo. Less of the poet's support comes from the general public than from the public treasury. How many poets make as much as $1,000 a year from the purchase of their works? Damn few. How many make ten or twenty times that from publicly subsidized readings, fellowships, academic positions, and editing periodicals? I should say nearly all of those we call "professional."

Moreover, at every stage of the journey, so many other poets are encountered crowding the same public highway, I had not thought death had undone so many. Poets are in competition for jobs, readings, publication. As Russell Banks recently wrote in the *American Writing Programs Newsletter,* "once again . . . we have a House that Jack Built—and Jack still means money, doesn't it?" Banks goes on: "This is the book written by the person who was the student of the person who edited the book for the student that got reviewed by the

---

[4]From *Praying Wrong: New and Selected Poems 1957–1984* (New York: Atheneum, 1984), p. 103.

[5]Ted Hughes, in the Introduction to *Johnny Panic and the Bible of Dreams,* by Sylvia Plath (New York: Harper and Row, 1979), pp. 2, 5.

colleague of the teacher who reviewed the book written by the colleague who hired the teacher to teach his students while he took a leave on the grant that was awarded by the panel on which the teacher sat as a replacement for the colleague who edited the anthology that included the work of the student who wrote the book." The gossip of contemporary poets has much less to do with sects or cults, or even with reviews and publications, than it does with readings and professorships and writing programs at colleges. Yet a mere forty years ago the creative writing major and the poet-in-residence hardly existed in American institutions—perhaps only at Bennington, Sarah Lawrence, Ann Arbor.

Could our society possibly have hamstrung poetry by transforming it from a calling into a profession? The question, though seldom asked and never crisply answered, is worth asking. Have we in some degree disarmed poets by cushioning them with the proceeds of the very technology that we all agree has tainted our perception of the poet's authenticity? And what effect does the new relation between the public sector of the economy and the poet's livelihood exert upon the poet's work? Could it be—could it possibly be—that we have relegated poets to a role as powerless as that of housewives gossiping across the back fence? And that we have done so by the same means we kept housewives at home, by putting them down and buying them off?

Unfortunately our poetry, like our fiction, has stumbled across a desperately genteel resistance inherent in the dirty little secrets of the twentieth century. In literature we may talk of sex as much as we like; we cannot bring ourselves to talk of money. If the novel, in the hands of Jane Austen and George Eliot, talked frankly of great expectations and livings and inheritances and marriage settlements, modernist literature and criticism hardly mention money seriously except in the works of the successors of Henry James and Edith Wharton, the matter-of-fact aristocrats Gore Vidal and Louis Auchincloss. Or without seriousness in the vulgarized genres of Harold Robbins and Judith Krantz, where the highest apotheosis known to humankind is to be featured on the cover of *People*. (Or in crime novels, where the apotheosis is to be featured on the wall of the Post Office.) In contemporary poetry the subject of money seldom turns up at all, though it was plentifully at hand in Homer and Horace and Shakespeare and Goethe. Wordsworth and Tennyson shooed it away in distaste.

Contemporary critical theory about poetry owes too much to psychology and not nearly enough to economics. Ezra Pound knew better (though not well enough) and blamed *usura*—a term that late in his life he would correct to the dear old deadly sin of Avarice. Pound's student and publisher, James Laughlin, has said that nowadays the prime interest rate has more effect on what is kept in print than literary taste does. But most of our critics, bristling at the very thought of technology, will blame all the ills of poetry on "computer language," on "cultural change," on poor old Science, and will harken back to an earlier age when all was simple and therefore all was well.

It might be healthy here to suggest that such dilemmas have long been familiar to those who are familiar with money, and to recall Marx's famous passage in *The Eighteenth Brumaire of Louis Napoleon:*

> Men make their own history, but they do not make it just as they please. . . . The tradition of all the dead generations weighs like a nightmare on the brain of the living. And . . . precisely in such periods of revolutionary crisis they anxiously conjure up the spirits of the past to their service and borrow from them names, battle cries and costumes in order to present the new scene of world history in this time-honored disguise and this borrowed language.

Likewise, Marshall McLuhan once wrote that yesterday's technology becomes today's art form. Pottery. Patchwork quilts. Letterpress printing. Harness-making. Poetry?

What would we find if we looked at the last great poetic revolution in English? Beginning arbitrarily in 1915 (the year Henry Holt published *North of Boston,* the year *Poetry* published "The Love Song of J. Alfred Prufrock" and "Sunday Morning"), we would find American poets revolutionizing their art by reaching back to the names, battle cries, and costumes of the past. Frost, recollecting *Lyrical Ballads* and the poet "speaking as a man to men," would summon up in the "sound of speech" a half-deserted New England landscape, "warming the frozen swamp as best it could / With the slow smokeless burning of decay." Pound, of whom Wyndham Lewis said, "there is almost nowhere in the Past that he has not visited," would raise his voice in medieval battle cries: "Damn it all! all this our South stinks peace." Stevens would dream his way into a calm unbroken past by trafficking in cathedrals and chinoiserie, a past remote from the present, impenetrable to the touch: "Death is the mother of beauty." And Eliot, shortly after, in 1919, would make his obeisance to the past, in "Tradition and the Individual Talent," by writing: "What is to be insisted upon is that the poet must develop or procure the consciousness of the past and that he should continue to develop this consciousness throughout his career."

Such poets, odd though their battle cries sound, were making a revolution in language and also a revolution in the place of poetry in society. They spoke not as a phalanx but as individuals individually aroused, each seeking a *point d'appui* through his own individual exertions and without recourse to any institution, public or private. That they looked to the past for support was integral to that revolution.

Today, contrarily, our poets are not up to revolution. The status quo is too important to them. Not only their lives but their works ignore the past, belittle the future. Vulgarizing Williams's motto, "no ideas but in things," they stick to the things they know: the present, the visible limits of their lives, the confines of their affairs. Even the tenses of their language reflect their commitment to the immediate present, to a world devoid of history. Influenced by half-understood translations from the Spanish (whose complex verb forms just won't fit into our language, the translators tell me), their rhetoric rolls around like a dog wriggling to scratch its back on the surface of the present indicative and the first person. The legacies of rhyme and meter are—or have until recently been—scoffed at like heresies; hypotactic syntax and grammatical complexity are regarded as obfuscation, too rusty to operate, "nostalgic," "old-fashioned." Such futures as those celebrated by

George Herbert, hailed by Mayakovsky, regarded as appalling by Mandelstam or apocalyptic by Thomas Hardy, seem to take no place either in the language or in the thought of the American poetry of the 1970s: for poets of this era the present is enough to get on with, to bog down in.

Could this imposition of the everyday, this emasculation of the possibilities of poetry, be the result of the way a society has put poetry in its place, having transformed it into a trade as prosaic and secure as any other, with wages, expectations, entitlements, medical insurance, retirement benefits, and industrial diseases? Have the tenets of fashion, of advertising, and of such journalism as *People, New York,* and *W* (none of which would think of publishing a line of poetry) been able once again to stifle true originality in poetry by concentrating on the gossip about poets' private lives and, if they mention their work at all, imposing the silly attitude that eighteenth-century contemporaries employed to belittle Bach—that art must be new to be true?

Yes. No. Of course not. Our most gifted and original poets do of course find their way back to the past and arm themselves to reinvent the language and strike out for the future. Obviously there are too few of these, but that has never been otherwise. Thomas Shadwell ("The rest to some faint reason make pretense, / But Shadwell never deviates into sense") was once poet laureate; Antonio Salieri, holding the patronizing power in the reign of Joseph II, held the means to destroy Mozart. Yet despite his worst efforts Mozart's music had the wherewithal to transcend Salieri, and Shadwell survives only in Dryden's "MacFlecknoe." Pushkin, within six years after Salieri's death, had written a play to illustrate the envy of mediocrity for genius, as Peter Shaffer did a century and a half later in *Amadeus*. Originality penetrates deeply into the past: it has no choice if it is to face itself and move forward. "The tradition of all the dead generations weighs like a nightmare on the brain of the living."

# The Great Predicament of Poetry

Robert Frost wrote in 1946: "Every poem is an epitome of the great predicament; a figure of the will braving alien entanglements."[1] This is as spirited a definition now as it was then. Of course entanglements vary, and each generation—indeed every poet of each generation—gets entangled in a different variety of alienation.

In recent years our younger poets, heeding Rilke's dangerous admonition, "You must change your life," have tried to alter their poetic gait by simplifying it to a walk—the immemorial process by which poetry repeatedly tries to purge itself of the past, of corruption, of the stilted or the venal. Device, decoration, and artifice go by the board. Rhyme and meter were long since cast out: "After Einstein," Denise Levertov once announced with Newtonian certainty, "such things are no longer possible."

Other traditional elements of verse have been thrown off like encumbering garments, as the more adventurous poets try to brave their ways through the jungle. Off with the balladlike elements of narrative, chorus, and refrain. Down with the incantatory inflammations of resonance and intonation. Leave singing to the rock howlers. Most confusingly and most recently, many of the younger American poets have at last thrown away their canteens, discarding the very structure of grammar and syntax that gave poetry its skele-

*The Atlantic Monthly,* June, 1979.
[1] Robert Frost, "The Constant Symbol," *The Atlantic Monthly* (October 1946), and in *Selected Prose of Robert Frost,* ed. Hyde Cox and Edward Connery Lathem (New York: Henry Holt, 1956), p. 25.

ton if it wished to utter anything more complex than simple outcry. The motives underlying this universal disarmament of the will are unclear. Why should poets attempt to brave alien entanglements without so much as a weapon or a stitch of clothing?

Many literary influences have urged poets into this enterprise of walking naked. The earliest was imagism, which has for several generations attracted poets to the intensity of the unadorned fact. "Say it," William Carlos Williams urged in the same year Robert Frost stated the Great Predicament, "no ideas but in things," and launched himself forthwith into his epic poem *Paterson,* that immortal shopping list. A second instigation to poetic streamlining was surrealism, with its amusing or desperate attempts to adjoin sequences of dissimilar objects, so that poetry could flash in the spaces between them, without allowing writer or reader any insight into the ways in which the iceberg might—or might not—have relations with the apple tree. The third and most recent influence, I think, was the impact on our poetry of translations, especially from such highly inflected Spanish poets as Lorca, Neruda, Vallejo, who take us into a country without borders, a landscape of intense self-awareness, a universe of solipsism conveyed in a huge complexity of statements contrary to fact. In translation the complexity of their Spanish subjunctives and conditionals fell away because English could not handle them.

Combine these literary influences with the social facts of postwar America, when most of our poets accepted residence in the university, where poetry is assembled in workshops that became connected to one another by a communications network of itinerant readaloud poets who provided instant oral *derniers cris* of poetic fashion. I notice in the work of a great many poets now under fifty a dismaying distrust of the more complex resources of our language. Having hacked their arms and legs away, they fight upon their stumps. In the poems submitted to *The Atlantic* at present, an editor can read for hours without encountering a poem couched in any tense but the present or employing any mood but the indicative. What is this chill in the air that keeps our poets confined to the interior facing in, or even, more solipsistic than that, transcribing their dreams onto paper and calling them poems because they sound funny? If Frost's definition may be tolerated, the cause may lie in a timidity of the will, or else in entanglements from a new and even more alien source, like that suggested in *Invasion of the Body Snatchers.*

But such generalizations, while valid enough, do not allow for the wide variety that contemporary poetry still offers. Some poets' natures, overriding mere technique, force them into a violent convulsion of the will. *Killing Floor,* by a poet who calls herself Ai, shows that she knows more about violence than most. Her first book, *Cruelty,* was vivid and shocking. Her second extends her appalling vision of life in poems that speak almost invariably in the present tense, in the voices of murderers, suicides, pimps and whores, drunks, conquistadores, rebels, bloodthirsty visionaries. They sound notes of death and self-destruction.

> You're damned in the cradle,
> in the grave, even in Heaven.
> Dying doesn't end anything.
> Get up. Swing those machetes.

> ("Pentecost")

Ai's poetry purges, like Kali the Destroyer. There is nothing ingratiating or "attractive" about it. She carries herself like a prophet, a priestess of blood. It is hard to know where such a line of work will take her, but she does not falter: her dedication seems complete. The nuances of language, when faced with such realities as those she wields, seem almost irrelevant; and her own language transparent to the forces expressed in it.

Geoffrey Hill, born in 1932, is English, which may account for the prevalence in his most recent book, *Tenebrae,* of some of the appurtenances of verse that have been abandoned, or never adopted, by his American coevals. Hill is not troubled by imagism or surrealism. Formal structures lend him a rhetorical force that free verse has to find for itself:

> The tributaries of the Sheaf and Don
> bulge their dull spate, cramming the poor bridges.
> ("An Apology for the Revival of Christian Architecture in
> England")

Hill's earlier *Mercian Hymns* confronted the State, an institution of his island; now, in *Tenebrae*, he confronts the Church. The heart of the book, perhaps, beats in two gorgeously written sonnet sequences, "Lachrymae," and "An Apology for the Revival of Christian Architecture in England." In an agony of denunciation he finds the churches empty of souls, empty of meaning, fated to corruption:

> the stony hunger of the dispossessed
> locked into Eden by their own demand.
> ("The Masque of Blackness")

> I founder in desire for things unfound.
> I stay amid the things that will not stay.
> ("Pavana Dolorosa")

The Spanish poetry that speaks to Hill is the grandeur of Lope de Vega and the Counter-Reformation rather than the agonies of the Spanish Republic. His complexities of rhyme, syntax, metaphor, grammar, and logical sequence display all the manners that seem to have been lacking in American poetry; yet his poems take some getting used to before the reader notices how subversive and pessimistic they are. But their taking the forms of traditional poetry is deeply purposeful, like entering a church in order to strip it of its treasures, of all hope. If these are poems of an empty and despairing Christian faith, they carry a certain conviction in their very structure: *Credo quia impossibile*. I believe in poetry because it is impossible, I believe because I must, because I am destined to play the role of helpless communicant. With all his Old World resources, Hill, like American poets, faces the Great Predicament. And when it comes to the crunch, he must fall back on tautologies: this is that, as that is actually this. The strain on language, which it cannot overcome by its own devices, makes the poet discover similarity, similes disguised, declaring it is, it *is,* it IS. Hill approaches the conclusion of his title poem, "Tenebrae," with just such an insistence:

> this is the chorus of obscene consent,
> this is a single voice of purest praise.

∾

If Geoffrey Hill's grandeur is noted for being difficult of access, Tess Gallagher, a young American, is as challenging in her own way. Her beautifully designed second book, *Under Stars,* shows her braving the most difficult of entanglements; unlike most other poets of her generation she faces up, in every line of her book, to the full engagement with language. She does not get stuck in tautologies. Her poems evince a syntactic regeneration, a renewed involvement with the processes and passage of time.

Gallagher's work requires enough alertness in the reader to follow her through facets of grammatical inclination, to listen with alertness for the rhythms and interaction of her syntactical groupings. Here is one characteristic passage, from a poem called "Second Language":

> The words come back.
> You are with yourself again
> as that child who gave up the spoon,
> the bed, the horse to its colors
> and uses. There is yet no hint
> they would answer to anything else
> and your tongue does not multiply the wrong,
> the stammer calling them back
> and back.
>
> You have started the one word
> again, again as though it had to be made
> a letter at a time
> until it mends itself into saying.

Relish, if you can, the nuances of that punctuation, the prepositions that alter the motion of the language as softly yet abruptly as billiard cushions, the shifts between one tense and mood and another, and the uses of the present tense to engorge the past, the past tenses to illuminate the present, the present tense (as in the last line) to forecast the future.

The apparent simplicity of Gallagher's way of speaking turns out to be difficult to follow because she is dodging through the most intricate of entanglements, the movements of the human mind itself. Who has decreed to our younger poets that the present is more immediate than the past and future, or even separate from them? Praise is due to the poet who manages to make them coexist in a single figure of the mind's action. Gallagher, to her credit, has undertaken the daunting poetic adventure of utilizing all the equipment of language to explore the nuances of feeling, the nature of the passage of time, and, most intricately and reflexively, the nature of language itself, through which we know most of those other things. Every poet has a vision, whether of violence or transcendence, the shadow in the picture, the decay of Christianity. Gallagher's vision, if she retains and enlarges it, will live in three or four dimensions, through the operation of her utterance in space and time. Poetry is, for her, most completely the subject of the poem.

# The Refuge of the Present Tense

*One escapes from all the anguish of this world*
*Into the refuge of the present tense.*
                        —Anthony Hecht, "The Venetian Vespers"

Why do so many readers of new poetry feel that something is missing? One could give a great variety of answers. Some would be unflattering to the reader, some to the poet. Let me concentrate on only one: the fashionable dominance of the present tense. Others have pointed to the prevalence of the present in contemporary fiction also, but perhaps three-quarters of all the new poetry that I read is cast in the present tense, indicative mood. Few poems show traces of the past emphatic ("In Xanadu did Kubla Khan / A stately pleasure-dome decree") or of the subjunctive mood ("Had we but world enough, and time, / This coyness, Lady, were no crime") or of the present perfect ("I have done it again. One year in every ten / I manage it") or of the simple past ("Because I could not stop for Death / He kindly stopped for me") or of the imperative mood ("At the round earth's imagin'd corners, blow / Your trumpets, Angells") or the future tense ("Shall I compare thee to a Summer's day?").

Many casual readers of today's poetry misunderstand their own discomfort at what they are reading and complain only of the absence of rhyme and meter. What really underlies their dissatisfaction, I think, is that so many contemporary poets lack conviction, and their weakness shows in their language. They have lost some degree of belief in the validity of poetic

*The Atlantic Monthly,* September, 1988, under the title "Time, Please."

utterance and consequently tend to mute their own voices. Readers in the nineteenth century flocked to poetry. Was it because poets then were confident of what they were saying? "There was a time when meadow, grove and stream, / The earth, and every common sight, / To me did seem / Apparell'd in celestial light, / The glory and the radiance of a dream." The present tense, in contrast, constrains us to hear only the voice of the watcher. The present indicative lets a poet stand a foot away from commitment, three to four feet away from identification, six feet away from declaration: "September silence sags over the field. / Faded summer denims flap with fatigue / on a neighbor's clothesline" (this instance comes from my own work). Contemporary poetry tends to cast the poet in the role of witness, even of clinician. Between the poet and the event falls a shadow: "The apparition of these faces in the crowd: / Petals on a wet, black bough." Pound's split, verb-less figure implies externality, irony, remoteness, alienation, impotence, inaction. It omits relationship, intimacy, inter-action, community, and the passage of time. Poems descended from it and composed in the present indicative encourage us to draw back lest we plunge in, like J. Alfred Prufrock. They enable us to avoid recommendation, passion, declaration. Speaking in the present tense says that everything is usual but nothing is special.

What of the poet's timeless roles: scribe, historian, cantor, prophet, musician, elegiast? The work of many contemporary poets suggests that they cannot respond to an invitation to participate in what they find alien. Their poems seem unable to imagine the actuality of absent or future hearers, and sound like letters slipped anonymously beneath a door. But let a poet move into one of the past or future tenses, and the reader may credit the writer's belief that what he says hap-pened happened, or that what will be will be.

"A poem may be worked over once it is in being," wrote Robert Frost, "but may not be worried into being. Its most precious quality will remain its having run itself and carried away the poet with it. Read it a hundred times: it will forever keep its freshness as a metal keeps its fragrance. It can never lose its sense of a meaning that once unfolded by surprise as it went."[1]

Hear the beauty of those verb tenses ringing against the weight of the nouns. Hear, too, the time dimension exfoliating in that last sentence. In such utterances we hear what is gone, for the moment, from most poetry. Poets must learn to believe again that time is their friend.

---

[1]"The Figure a Poem Makes," *Complete Poems of Robert Frost* (New York: Henry Holt, 1949), p. viii.

# The Perils of Reputation

Poets are peculiar plants, and nobody knows much about what makes them germinate. As W. H. Auden, in his role as Professor of Poetry at Oxford, once declared, "Whatever his future life as a wage-earner, a citizen, a family man may be, to the end of his days his life as a poet will be without anticipation. He will never be able to say: 'Tomorrow I will write a poem and, thanks to my training and experience, I already know I shall do a good job.' In the eyes of others a man is a poet if he has written one good poem. In his own he is only a poet at the moment when he is making his last revision to a new poem. The moment before, he was still only a potential poet; the moment after, he is a man who has ceased to write poetry, perhaps forever."[1]

The poet's task is somehow to keep his talent watered without knowing where the seed lies. If poets' lives have often seemed irregular, they have taken that shape from the poet's nervous, even frantic, attempts to keep the source of his poetry deep, dark, fertile, and accessible. Nothing frightens a poet so much as the prospect or the knowledge that he has lost the way to his own poetry, for it turns the knife in his awareness that he has lost the way back to his own youth, when poetry welled up spontaneously. Dylan Thomas seems to have been haunted by the fear that he would go dry—and he kept himself very wet, perhaps as insurance. Some poets among

_The Atlantic Monthly,_ January, 1966, under the title "The Gilt Edge of Reputation."
[1]W. H. Auden, _The Dyer's Hand and Other Essays_ (New York: Random House, 1962), p. 41.

those who teach used to try to brace themselves by a devotion to criticism, editing, instruction; but poetry is a bit uneasy in the same room with Literature and may even bolt.

Yet, though we are fascinated by the war between poetry and its rivals for attention, we ought not to forget that poetry has a life and strength that we have been able to count on. It lasts. Shakespeare was clearly right about the relative unreliability of marble and the gilded monuments of princes, and bets will be gladly taken in this quarter that Robert Lowell's 1959 poem "For the Union Dead" will outlast the Boston skyscrapers planted in the same year. Poetry lasts because it is rooted deep, and this is one reason why its practitioners are so profoundly attached that its withering can sometimes cause death—at least the death of personality. Through poetry they retain touch with the sources of their being.

The poet requires the roots; the student of poetic acclaim sees only the flower, especially when the poetry is new. For a poet's reputation to last he must be not only good but lucky. A poet's work may win sudden fame for the same reason as the topless bathing suit, for what it discloses; what is hidden may not emerge until later, and in private. A news-hungry cultural editor may find it "symptomatic of the times." The English departments may find it consorts with their current curricula. The poet may inadvertently stumble into celebrity as an exile, a martyr, or an example of misbehavior.

T. S. Eliot, in the 1940s, became the sudden focus of academic attention and was read, on assignment, by every puzzled English student in America. Ten or fifteen years later the same fate befell Wallace Stevens. The magnificent but no less scrutable poetry of Thomas Hardy, on the other hand, has been in perennial repute without ever having been overrated or much assigned. One thing is clear about the reputation of living poets: there is room for only so many growth stocks on the market at one time. Frost's popularity receded in the forties with the rise of Eliot's star, but as Eliot ceased writing and Frost lived on to a great old age, Frost's stock rose again, assisted of course, by Presidential Favor.

Pound, Eliot, and others contributed inestimably to the language of poetry, and their reputations thrived as a result. It would be a mistake to follow the common belief that the peculiar nature of the twentieth century can be captured exclusively through innovations of form. Edwin Muir could hardly have been less interested in technical and linguistic innovation; yet Muir, at once the translator of Kafka and the interpreter of the Scottish ballad, managed to fill his rurally imagined poetry with the nightmare and anxiety of the twentieth century. His reputation never swelled out of size, but he was one of the most penetrating of interpreters, and his vision went the deeper for being couched in a language as old as the hills and animals of his poems.

In the 1950s Dylan Thomas's American readings and cautionary fate boosted his quotations. His vocal and other performances engaged a following that had no reason to be attracted by any other poet and was not tempted to name rock groups and singers after better-behaved bards. William Carlos Williams was never published at all in England until after his death in 1964. Posterity is a harsh mistress. She punishes poets like Erasmus Darwin or Charles Churchill or Alfred Austin for taking excessive pains with contemporary issues or poets like William Cullen Bryant or Arthur Hugh Clough for ignoring them. Then she can reward Milton or Herrick for exactly the same reasons. A good poet's reputation grows in the long run in spite of itself, yet not without reference to reality, like the easy neighborhood girl who has slept with more men than most people know but not as many as some people think.

At this moment Robert Graves looks more like pure poet than anyone else alive—this in spite of the fact that among living poets he has written more prose than anyone else: novels, essays, scholarly polemics, criticism, and translations—all in their way just as much *his* as his poems. His verses, however, take place in an archetypical world all their own. They have in recent years had no subjects except love. Love, of course, encompasses its allies and its betrayals: treachery, fidelity, the dreadful intimacy as well as the delights imposed upon love's slaves, the appalling services required of the devotee. Yet, while the poems speak of love, the poet is always speaking of something else: of the Muse's magic, of service to the White

Goddess. Graves alone among contemporary poets seems to live, as Coleridge did, in a world of naked-breasted sirens and reptilian enemies, of substitutions and transformations, in the universe of metaphor.

In his latest book, *Man Is, Woman Does,* Graves combines this phantasmagoria with an extraordinary flexibility of rhythm. Listen to "The Dance of Words":

> But see they dance it out again and again
> Until only lightning is left to puzzle over—
> The choreography plain, and the theme plain.

And in another, addressed as ever to his Muse, he states the aesthetic desire again:

> Teach me a measure of casualness
> Though you stalk into my room like Venus naked.

"The theme plain." "A measure of casualness." It would seem to come only to the mature. Yeats turned toward simplicity, and Graves, and Eliot, and, more recently, Robert Lowell and Elizabeth Bishop. But plainness of manner can only be a bore if there is no lightning to puzzle over. For many years Graves's output was slender but intense, five poems a year, he once said. Now the stream is swollen and even growing turbid. Hardly a year goes by but he gives us another collection. In *Man Is, Woman Does* the sections are already prudently numbered for the next edition of his *Collected Poems*. The pressure to write has evidently become dangerous, as witness "A Last Poem":

> A last poem, and a very last, and yet another—
> O, when can I give over?
> Must I drive the pen until blood bursts from my nails
> And my breath fails and I shake with fever,
> Or sit well-wrapped in a many-coloured cloak
> Where the moon shines new through Castle Crystal?
> Shall I never hear her whisper softly:
> "But this is truth written by you only,
> And for me only; therefore, love, have done?"

Radical, nihilist, lover, parodist, Anglo-Catholic, pastoralist, saint, schoolmarm, W. H. Auden has successively and simultaneously acted all these roles, while never for long relinquishing what seems to me his favorite one: that of Satan or his advocate, courteous and outrageous, standing on a high place at the reader's elbow and gesturing toward the cities of the plain below. He asks questions so pointed, offers temptations so ingenious, that the answers and refusals come hard. From the early revolutionary poems that galvanized a left-wing generation, to the great elegies on Yeats and Freud and the outbreak of war ("O all the instruments agree / The day of his death was a dark cold day." "To us he is no more a person / Now but a whole climate of opinion." "I sit in one of the dives / On Fifty-second street / Uncertain and afraid / As the clever hopes expire / Of a low dishonest decade"), to the quizzical ingenuities of *The Sea and the Mirror* and *The Age of Anxiety,* to the Christian paradoxes of *For the Time Being,* to his most perfect volumes, *Nones* and *The Shield of Achilles,* Auden has moved through wave after wave of reputation. Some of those who were tickled by his early outrageousness later turned away in political disgust as the role of deacon took over; others tired of the wagging forefinger or the wicked gleam in the eye. Others who at first were irritated by his cleverness have become impressed with his wisdom. He himself has faltered. *Homage to Clio* seemed to me a considerable falling off; but the newest book, *About the House,* is full of exalted achievements, especially in the first half, called "Thanksgiving for a Habitat." Auden's disguise in this cycle is that of Clever Chap, beneath which he hides an immense reserve of humanity, sympathy, and good feeling. He is capable of the old wit:

> Lifted off the potty,
> Infants from their mothers
> Hear their first impartial
> Words of worldly praise:
> Hence, to start the morning
> With a satisfactory
> Dump is a good omen
> All our adult days.

The Clever Chap is archaeologist, anthropologist, psychologist, engineer, linguist (a reader like me, who must depend on a mere *Webster's Unabridged,* loses his footing among some of the terms Auden trots out from the recesses of *The Oxford Dictionary*—*depatical, flosculent, neotene, dowly, ubity*), but beyond his other roles, he is always poet, and seldom before has so much information been converted from dross to gold. From under the surface moral veins keep emerging, as in this postscript to the poem on the study, a lovely elegy to the late Louis MacNeice:

> Time has taught you
>         how much inspiration
> your vices brought you,
>         what imagination
> can owe temptation
>         yielded to,
> that many a fine
>         expressive line
> would not have existed,
>         had you resisted . . .
> You hope, yes,
>         your books will excuse you,
> save you from hell:
>         nevertheless . . .
>         God may reduce you
> On Judgment Day
>         to tears of shame,
> reciting by heart
>         the poems you would
> have written, had
>         your life been good.

If Graves writes in the role of the helpless Lover, and if Auden is the Clever Chap, Elizabeth Bishop is the Expatriate, and she writes with an expatriate's simple confidence about her homes, the adopted Brazil, the native American and Canadian Northeast, the visits to Florida. With the opening lines of the opening poem, "Arrival at Santos," in *Questions of Travel,* we are in knowing hands:

> Here is a coast; here is a harbor;
> here, after a meager diet of horizon, is some scenery:
> impractically shaped and—who knows?—self-pitying
>     mountains,
> sad and harsh beneath their frivolous greenery . . .

What a lovely movement in the verse! What self-confidence in that "who knows?" (*She* does.) How she conveys that sense of unfamiliarity at the end of a voyage, when land seems artificial and somehow more personable than land has any right to be. Her book shimmers with clear-eyed observation, absolute and lovely simplicity, and a gentle flickering humor. Take the opening of a poem called "Twelfth Morning; or What you Will":

> Like a first coat of whitewash when it's wet,
> the thin gray mist lets everything show through:
> the black boy Balthazár, a fence, a horse,
>     a foundered house,
>
> —cement and rafters sticking from a dune.
> (The Company passes off these white but shopworn
> dunes as lawns.) "Shipwreck," we say; perhaps
>     this is a housewreck.

The poem as a whole is one of description and transformation, showing objects and events transformed by the morning of Epiphany; but the unforeseen shifts in rhythm and point of view arouse the possibility of expectation and make the poem itself, and its transformations, work their changes. The reader cannot see the events of the morning unless he is kept off balance, and the poet has taken pains to keep him so.

The clarity and the level, humorous gaze of Elizabeth Bishop's poems give them not only their poetic charm but their unpretentious profundity. Sometimes—and this may be one of those cases—it is the very way of speaking that transcends the artificial forces that regulate reputation. Some reputations grow naturally and never wither.

# In Quest to Have Extreme

*Madness & booze, madness & booze.*
*Which'll can tell who preceded whose?*
*What chicken walked out on what egg?*
—John Berryman, *The Dream Songs*, no. 225

The great American poets who were born in the nineteenth century and came of age around the First World War lived a very long time. Conrad Aiken, who died in 1973, was the last survivor of the titanic group that included Pound, Eliot, Frost, Stevens, Ransom, Williams, Jeffers, Marianne Moore, and Cummings. This climax forest cast a heavy shadow over the younger growth beneath, but nonetheless another generation took seed in the shade, born during the darkness of the First World War and not ready to come of age as poets until after the Second. With the early death of Robert Lowell in 1977 the poets of this compact generation—academically trained, Europe-oriented, interlaced by personal and professional ties—passed out of life, leaving behind a handful of their peers, dears, elders, and teachers: Elizabeth Bishop, Stanley Kunitz, Robert Penn Warren, and a cadre of poets younger than themselves, including Richard Wilbur, Howard Nemerov, and May Swenson, with a gaggle of others, all born in the 1920s, talents too gifted and numerous to mention here.

The senior poets, as well as the juniors, were perhaps luckier than the war-born. Luckier not only in living longer, but luckier in finding the power to work magnificently into old

Written 1977–90 and not previously published.

age, as Warren and Kunitz so notably did. It could be that the lack of extremity is what made this possible. The poets born during the First World War pushed poetry to the edge of tolerance, as they maltreated their lives. We are unlikely ever to succeed in answering the question: was it a matter of choice, or destiny? They sought to cure the ills of life with poetry, and, whatever their successes, they failed in that.

My first full-time job, begun in 1950 when I was twenty-two, was as a first reader at Harcourt, Brace and Company, as it was then called. It brought me face to face with poets poets poets, not only those aspirants my own age, hauling in manuscripts hoping for publication, but the old giants. T. S. Eliot turned up one day, with his deacon's white handkerchief peering from the sleeve of his black coat, and his mellifluous how-do-you-do. I was once given Wallace Stevens's benevolent hand to shake at a large gathering and looked up into the ruddy mask of his face and down at the portly swag of his belly. Carl Sandburg often worked in rolled-up shirtsleeves in a corner of the Harcourt, Brace offices, polluting the atmosphere with his cheap cigar smoke and his donkey laughter. E. E. Cummings, ivory skull glowing like a nimbus around his sensuous face, visited the office, as did young lookalike Richard Wilbur: handsome, poised, self-sufficient, like Cummings seemingly at ease with his beauty. So hierarchic were the poetic reputations of the time that only the visit of Eliot (just turned sixty and the latest American Nobel Laureate in Literature) ranked as an Office Event, with secretaries goggling over the top of five-foot partitions toward the parade-route that led to Robert Giroux's office. Bob was then Harcourt's editor-in-chief, resembling nearly no other editor-in-chief of this century in his dedication to poetry, and presiding over one of the great lists in American publishing history.

But I remember another visit, more dissonant than the chance to gawk at Eliot. One mid-morning in 1954 the atmosphere was breached by the wild sounds of desperate laughter as two young men, talking very loudly, passed unheeding by the receptionist and struck a wavering course toward Giroux's office. With them, their usher in a cape, scurried Catharine Carver, the assiduous editor who shared my cubicle, attempting to steer Robert Lowell and John Berryman toward their destination, not, clearly, an easy chore. The two men had been making a night of it, and both looked seedy and sounded strident. Lowell's nasal whine carried well enough, but not so effectively as Berryman's hollering, until the door of Giroux's sanctum closed behind them, and somehow silence descended.

I had my own reasons for being frightened of drunken men; but my reaction to this apparition went deeper than genteel anxiety. By their scruffy foray into the bourgeois office setting, these poets were announcing something about themselves. Clearly confident of their powers ("John, we used the language as if we made it"),[1] they also seemed by their very carriage (Lowell's hulking and crabwise, Berryman's splayed and shambling) to be declaring a sort of heedless vulnerability in body and in mind. They disdained to wear any disguise, no deacon's coat or Hartford spiffiness or Chicago stogie, no good looks or good manners, just to be poets, in their youth, "had, having, and in quest to have extreme."

Other poets, younger than they, seemed to have different matters on their minds, and only some (such as Allen Ginsberg, Anne Sexton, Sylvia Plath, W. D. Snodgrass, James Wright, eventually Adrienne Rich) lifted the curtain between the self and the world—the curtain that Berryman and Lowell had long since disdained to wrap themselves in. That curtain had on another occasion been thrown back for me when I heard Randall Jarrell, lisping and nasal through his beard, hilariously merciless, speaking of Goethe at Brandeis University, flushing out and shooting down the fumbling inquiries of the "question period" like a blue-ribbon duck hunter. In the recessional of the Fugitive tradition, among the ferment of the visually oriented poets of New York or the pharmacologically oriented poets of San Francisco or the Swedenborgian poets of the Upper Midwest, arguments were in progress, debates were being waged, fury was at work. Nonetheless, for

---

[1] Robert Lowell, *History* (New York: Farrar, Straus and Giroux, 1973), p. 203.

me at the outset of my work as a writer, the awesome leaders of the chase were the poets born in the first war.

The year 1963—a year that saw the deaths not only of nineteenth-century Robert Frost and William Carlos Williams, but the far less timely deaths of Theodore Roethke (b. 1908) and Sylvia Plath (b. 1932)—signalled the coming of more thunderheads. Roethke's poetry had been darkening for two decades with the lightning of compassion and the thunder of madness; Plath's, with the more sinister thunder of rage and dispossession. Robert Frost had once told me of a black night at Bread Loaf when he had heard Lowell and Roethke stumbling together up the path toward his cottage, egging each other on with cries of "Come on, manic!" "Come on, manic!" In 1963 such stories were still a bit of a joke, even after Robert Lowell's repeated drastic hospitalizations, which began in 1949. But after a long history of mental illness, Roethke was the first to die—of heart failure one afternoon in a Seattle swimming pool. He had been a friend of Kunitz, Lowell, Berryman, Louise Bogan, Dylan Thomas. Perhaps more significant, unlike most of the major American poets born in the nineteenth century, Roethke had been a teacher, and a devoted one, the first of the great writing teachers, at Lafayette, Penn State, Bennington, and the University of Washington. Though often hospitalized and often drunk, he had pressed poems on toward the "far field" of his childhood, a glassed-in paradise of unfettered sensibility, and he had listened back through the generations to "Smart, and Blake, and that sweet man, John Clare," for the sound, the sense, and the nonsense of poetry. Roethke's Yeatsian verse was not particularly "confessional," but his life was given to the quest to have extreme: his teaching gave him so much anxiety that he regularly lost his breakfast before teaching a class; while, in his seizures of madness, he would imagine himself a tycoon, barking Buy! and Sell! into a telephone, which his warders had considerately disconnected.

Randall Jarrell, Robert Lowell wrote, once said "bitterly and lightheartedly that 'the gods who had taken away the poet's audience had given him students.' " Perhaps the most person-

ally demanding and intellectually instructive of his genera-
tion, Jarrell, like Lowell a student of Ransom and Robert
Penn Warren (in whose English class he used to hiss and
sneer at the less intelligent responses of his fellow-freshmen),
eventually became one of Lowell's teachers. As a poet he had
less concern than other poets of his generation in trying to
find "his own" voice, but sought for other voices, often the
voices of women, in which to speak his poems. In "The
Woman at the Washington Zoo" or "The Lost World" Jarrell
moved in his maturing years toward a poetry of compassion,
of sorrowful striving, as in the mournful voice in which he
intoned his heartbreaking mimesis. "A mockingbird," he
wrote, "can sound like anything. / He imitates the world he
drove away. . . ."

His reciprocated admiration of Lowell had not prevented
Jarrell from taking a very different course from his friend.
Obsessed by literature, he emulsified his central concern with
languages, tennis, sport cars, and high-fidelity music. That
did not, however, tone him down. For one thing, as Lowell
wrote, "Although he was almost without vices, heads of col-
leges and English departments found his frankness more un-
settling and unpredictable than the drunken explosions of
some divine *enfant terrible,* such as Dylan Thomas." He also
quotes Jarrell as saying, "If I were a rich man, I would pay
money for the privilege of being able to teach."

This generation of American poets, then, like no other before
them, was given to the necessities and perils of teaching poets
about writing poetry. In the late fifties Lowell was a dominat-
ing if unstable presence in Boston, teaching at Boston Univer-
sity and, more than once, teetering over the edge of mental
illness before the very eyes of his students, some of whom—
Anne Sexton, Sylvia Plath—were similarly endangered. In
later years he regularly spent a couple of days a week teaching
poetry to a strongly bonded circle of acolytes at Harvard.
When poets and professors met around the circuit, they
would ask, with a dark and cozy confidentiality, "How *is* Cal
Lowell?" It was like asking for a weather report that had some-
how been suppressed in the papers. Was Lowell hospitalized

or not? Which stage of his manic-depressive cycle had recently been noted? But he was a *teacher,* if of a strange kind:

> To hear him read one's own words in his deep voice, inimitably blending Eastern aristocrat and Southern drawl, words intoned through a mask at times weary, puckish, or mad, was a bit of instant Olympus. His comments, with their sting of truth, were always tactfully sugarcoated. "Ah think that's almost perfect . . . of its *kind,*" he would breathe, leaving us to brood over what that "kind" might be. He would go over the poems word by word, line by line. "You've got to *load* the line," he would murmur, pushing his palms outward with graceful emphasis. With a grimace over a poem too blatant, he would advise, "Murk it up. . . ."
>
> If Lowell viewed us with benevolent disinterest, the ambitious graduate students and already published poets who attended his open office hours afforded a different perspective. . . . The atmosphere, as heavy with intrigue and animosity as a Jacobean drama, was frightening for me and the undergraduates who entered in. . . . Everyone vied for Lowell's approval; no one ever publicly questioned his judgment. . . . But what about Lowell's comment, repeated to me by a friend, that it was odd how almost all *good* women poets were either divorced or lesbian?[2]

Meanwhile Roethke in Seattle was marrying, convivially writing his expansive, visionary "mad" poems ("What's madness but nobility of soul / At odds with circumstance?") while Delmore Schwartz, destined to serve as the model for *Humboldt's Gift,* a book more widely read than all his own poetry, unable to obtain or retain a teaching job, was degenerating into alcoholic paranoia in New York, gradually avoided by his friends and publishers alike, and producing work of increasing incoherence. (I was one of the editors with whom he conducted an untidy correspondence during this period. It scared me, and I soon found ways to end it.)

---

[2]Celia Gilbert, "The Sacred Fire," in *Working It Out: 23 Women Writers, Artists, Scientists, and Scholars Talk about Their Lives and Work,* ed. Sara Ruddick and Pamela Daniels (New York: Pantheon Books, 1977), p. 313.

Berryman, now at Princeton or Minnesota, changing wives with some constancy, broke a long silence in 1964 with a Mississippi flood of dream songs, a spate of sixteen-line, harrowingly personal poems wilder than Robert Lowell's confessional ground-breaker, *Life Studies* (1959), more generous in sweep than Sylvia Plath's still unpublished *Ariel* (1966 in the United States). Lowell, in the later 1960s, began to reply to Berryman in fourteen-line verses, "unrhymed sonnets," in a pair of ostentatiously incompleted volumes both called *Notebook.* Schwartz succumbed in 1966 to a heart attack, accidentally locked out of his room in a seedy New York hotel while removing garbage in the middle of the night, and Jarrell, after a deep depression, died suddenly, hit by a car in 1965 on a dark road in Chapel Hill: perhaps it was an accident. "Jarrell's death was the sadder," Lowell wrote later, in comparison with Berryman's. "If it hadn't happened, it wouldn't have happened."

Both Lowell and Berryman wrote them obituaries. "Honest and cruel, peace now to his soul," wrote Berryman about Jarrell (Dream Song 121).[3] "They come this path, old friends, old buffs of death," wrote Lowell about Jarrell (*History,* p. 135). "Richard & Randall, & one who never did, / two who will never cross this sea again, / & Delmore . . . / the wind blows hard from our past into our future / and we are that wind, except that the wind's nature / was not to last," wrote Jarrell about the others (Dream Song 282). "Ah, the swift vanishing of my older / generation," wrote Lowell (including himself with the others) "—deaths, suicide, madness / of Roethke, Berryman, Jarrell and Lowell" (*History,* p. 204).

Berryman, obsessed by his father's suicide all his life, dashed off obituaries for every poet who died in his time and some who did not. For nearly a year in 1971 he managed to forswear the bottle, seeking instead some of the consolations of religion, drying out in hospitals and AA, as he described it in his posthumous novel *Recovery* (1973), and attempting to gather his waning and tattered forces for the future. But, like

---

[3]John Berryman, *The Dream Songs* (New York: Farrar, Straus and Giroux, 1969).

the princess who could not abide the pea under her mattress, peace would not come to him, and in his weak moment booze reached out and resumed possession. There had always been one other way out, as he had written many times: "Save us from shotguns & fathers' suicides. / It all depends on who you're the father *of* / if you want to kill yourself—" (Dream Song 235). Despite students, friends, wife, children (one only seven months old), poetry, and religion, he walked out to the high bridge over the Mississippi connecting two portions of the University of Minnesota campus in January, 1972, waved to a passerby, and hurled himself onto the shattering ice far below.

Robert Lowell, political/historical/tragical, leaving Boston in 1960 to take up residence in New York, and leaving New York in 1970 to take up residence in Great Britain, had begun in the sixties to play the game of literary power broker, in parallel to Roethke's fantasies of tycoon and gangster. "On my great days of sickness, I was God," he wrote (*History*, p. 139). His extraordinarily devoted, yet hard-headed wife, Elizabeth Hardwick, was well situated as one of the founding magnates of the *New York Review of Books*, but this association was not a new advantage for Lowell: at every decade of his adult life he seemed to link up with some review or other: the *Kenyon*, the *Southern*, the *Partisan*, the *New York*, the *New*. Lowell's books of the early sixties, *For the Union Dead* and *Near the Ocean*, showed a resurgence of his obsession with power, the power-hunger that had made him as a child play with armies of lead soldiers and pore over the lives of Napoleon's marshals. In the two versions of *Notebook* pouring out during the late sixties, he was revising toward the grandiose statements he would make about power in *History*, a book which would include reams of almost self-congratulatory obituaries along with bouts of self-laceration.

In 1968, Lowell had manically stumped the country as a visible part of Eugene McCarthy's presidential campaign. Who is to say whether Jarrell or Roethke, neither especially political, would have risen as Lowell did to the crises of the Civil Rights Movement and the horrors of the Vietnam era? For the decade after that political hegira, Lowell's work moved back and forth between the mode of personal confession, going so far as to quote and even rewrite personal letters from his wives and friends and his daughter into poems of his own, and rise, sometimes eloquently, into the mode of historical loftiness, ranging from Genesis to the present. His health became more and more shaky, his mental seizures less and less amenable to the lithium sulfate he had for so many years depended on for stability, his personal life more and more agonized, as he fathered a child in England by his third wife, Caroline Guinness, yet kept being drawn back to Elizabeth Hardwick, his second, in New York. He died of natural causes, if you can call it that, in a taxicab bound from Kennedy airport to Elizabeth Hardwick's house in Manhattan. When the driver arrived at the destination, he found his passenger dead in the back seat, along with an item of packaged sculpture.

The poets of this desperate generation were in their work all obsessed by the panoply of Europe, like Henry James and T. S. Eliot before them. Schwartz absorbed the Russian-Jewish radical tradition; Lowell staged poem after poem at the western edge of the Atlantic, looking east, from "The Quaker Graveyard at Nantucket" to "The Dolphin," and died at the western edge of the Atlantic, homeward bound. Berryman spent some of his last years in Ireland; Jarrell loved the German language and translated *Faust* and the Brothers Grimm. Roethke spent time in England, Ireland, and Rome, but seems to have looked more congenially homeward and to have settled with almost athletic satisfaction for the American experience, but he, like Jarrell, died before the disruptions of the 1960s had got fully under way.

Lowell, as surviving spokesman of his immediate contemporaries, and more than any, looked on America as a continent cursed by the angry God of Jonathan Edwards. He was also a passionate historian who, unlike most historians, paid as much attention to the losers in the game of history as the winners, especially after a friend had warned him, "Do you only suffer for other famous people, / and socially comforting non-entities?" (*History*, p. 182). Student of the past, he was also a prophet for the future.

Lowell suffered for his friends, and the loss of his friends: Roethke (1963), Jarrell (1965), Schwartz (1966), Berryman (1972). He himself, before dying in 1977, tried to send one last obituary consolation to Berryman: "We asked to be obsessed with writing, / and we were"[4] in a poem in which he claimed kinship:

> Yet really we had the same life,
> the generic one
> our generation offered
> (*Les Maudits*—the compliment
> each American generation
> pays itself in passing). . . .

*Madness & booze, madness & booze.* This generation of brother-poets had at least these two poisons in common. We have reason to think that their poetry, the best of it, will age wonderfully and probably as long as the language does, but the terrible question that none of them ever found a way to answer conveys the secret they all kept close: the dangers of poetry:

> Is getting well ever an art,
> or art a way to get well?[5]

("Unwanted")

---

[4]Robert Lowell, *Day by Day* (Farrar, Straus and Giroux, 1977), p. 27.
[5]*Day by Day,* p. 124.

# The Great Grassy World from Both Sides: The Poetry of Robert Lowell and James Dickey at Mid-Career

Americans are haunted by the dream of landing on an inhospitable coast, settling along the shore, looking alternately forward to the west into a vast hostile continent and backward over the shoulder to a bleak but necessary sea. The cities of the Old World (Sodom, Rome, London, and the constellations of guilt and terror that were Africa) always lay to the east. Even now our Westerners speak of The East with more wariness than of other points of the compass.

The openness of the American spirit, on the other hand, has always been sought in the opposite direction ("to the land vaguely realizing westward," as Frost had it), though our standards and our limitations come to us as the legacy of the Old World. "Have the elder races halted?" Walt Whitman asked. "Do they droop and end their lesson, wearied over there beyond the seas? / We take up the task eternal, and the burden, and the lesson / Pioneers! O Pioneers!"

The sea behind us has served in the office of a moat, but, more importantly, as our "connection" (the unconscious meanings are resonant) with the "mother country." Of course we transformed what we inherited. Look at the difference, for example, between the roles played by the sea in British and

*The Atlantic Monthly,* October, 1967, under the title "The Difficulties of Being Major." Revised in 1971 and published in *James Dickey: The Expansive Imagination,* ed. Richard J. Calhoun (Deland, Fla.: Everett-Edwards, 1973).

American legend and language. Over here our pirates were cowboys; our rebellious youths ran away to the Sea of Grass; and the only American marine adventurers who stirred our imagination were whalers and the clipper-shipmen of the China Trade, pressing on toward the setting sun before our Civil War.

With this continent at our face and that ocean at our back, we were from the beginnings of our national identity over-whelmed by the very scale of our situation and preoccupied with a massiveness that has pervaded most of our literary aspirations. The Revolution was greeted with an infestation of epic poetry, unread and unreadable; the first flowering of our fiction produced demands for the Great American Novel; Emerson denigrated "the courtly muses of Europe"; American criticism could not come of age in its own eyes until our scholars had nominated a pantheon of Major American Writers and hoisted them into niches to dominate the new courses and textbooks in American Literature. Since 1945 the demand for major writers has increased until, every publishing season, critics pick over each crop with the concentration of cannery workers grading fruit.

Not that the insistence on being "major" has much real meaning unless you are in search of a Goethe or a Dante. Yet it has affected American writers' notions of themselves and thus of the way they write. The career of Norman Mailer has been, both in his own eyes and those of his readers, a series of lunges toward Major Status. We can remember before him similar maneuverings on behalf of James Baldwin and Saul Bellow and John Barth and even James Gould Cozzens. Fiction in America is haunted by gigantism. In poetry, however, the rise and fall of reputations respond to different forces. Mere size in poetry is not necessary evidence of majority. Perhaps fortunately, there are few objective standards. W. H. Auden, in a characteristic mixture of pedagogy and insight, once set down some suggestive "rules" in the preface to his *Nineteenth Century British Minor Poets.*

One cannot say that a major poet writes better poems than a minor; on the contrary the chances are that, in the course of his lifetime, the major poet will write more bad poems than the minor. . . . To qualify as major, a poet, it seems to me, must satisfy about three and a half of the following five conditions.

1. He must write a lot.
2. His poems must show a wide range in subject matter and treatment.
3. He must exhibit an unmistakable originality of vision and style.
4. He must be a master of verse technique.
5. In the case of all poets we distinguish between their juvenilia and their mature work, but [the major poet's] process of maturing continues until he dies.[1]

Although Auden himself clearly satisfies at least four of these conditions, he is not a native American and, no doubt for that reason, he omits one additional criterion that most American-born poets would probably put at the top of their lists in one form or another: the major poet tries harder, is more ambitious, more "serious," has a sense of hugeness and grandeur. Auden feels no urge to dominate a continent.

Two of the American poets who could be considered in the running to pass Auden's tests today are Robert Lowell and James Dickey. In most respects they are as different as American poets can be. Lowell is a son of New England; Dickey, of the South. Lowell comes from and makes much of one of America's great aristocratic families; Dickey writes as a Populist without politics. Lowell looks constantly to the civilized past—to Rome both pagan and Christian, to the puritan ethic and the puritan neuroses, to the city both in Europe and America, to the dramatic aspects of poetry, to the sound of voices, to the tradition of Coleridge and Matthew Arnold and T. S. Eliot. Dickey, no less formidably learned than Lowell, carries the literary past more lightly, but his poems explore our overgrown frontier of archetypal scenes and situations; they deal with animals and hunting, with war and wounds, with drowning and flying, with domestic life rather

---

[1]W. H. Auden, ed., *Nineteenth Century British Minor Poets* (New York: Delacorte Press, 1966), pp. 15–16.

than family history, with pantheism rather than Catholicism, with death and transfiguration rather than funerals, with transformations of shapes and states-of-being rather than with the damage wrought by time and society. In form Lowell leans toward the elegy, the dramatic monologue, the verse play, while Dickey prefers the dithyramb, the narrative, the sermon. Lowell looks to the Atlantic Ocean and across it, Dickey to the great American wilderness and the continent within.

Robert Lowell has been publishing work of the first quality for over twenty years, and he has received ample recognition almost from the start. A privately printed volume, *Land of Unlikeness* (1944), was soon followed by *Lord Weary's Castle* (1946), which, incorporating the earlier volume, was soon awarded the Pulitzer Prize. Lowell was barely thirty. *Lord Weary's Castle* is notable not only for the force and intensity of the poems it contains but for the complexity and variety with which it echoes the literary and cultural assumptions of the day. These years just after World War II were the heyday of American Studies in the universities, of a self-conscious literary nationalism. *Lord Weary's Castle,* despite its Scottish title, was full of allusions to the principal figures and settings of the Massachusetts literary tradition: Jonathan Edwards, Hawthorne, Melville (the Melville of *Moby-Dick* and *Billy Budd*), Salem, New Bedford, Nantucket, Boston, and graveyards, graveyards, graveyards. The New England of this book and the next, *The Mills of the Kavanaughs* (1951), was a bleak helpless landscape filling up with the dead and memories of the dead. The puritan ethic and its failures were contrasted violently with the presence everywhere in the poems of the Roman Catholic ritual, for in those days Lowell had been received into the Catholic faith and had not yet left it.

Heaven and earth showed themselves in the repeatedly opposed symbols of the rainbow and the whale, those lightest and heaviest of things. "Atlantic, you are fouled with the blue sailors, / Sea-monsters, upward angel, downward fish." The violence and terror that have always lain at the heart of Lowell's poetry were there in plenty:

The bones cry for the blood of the white whale,
The fat flukes arch and whack about its ears,
The death-lance churns into the sanctuary, tears
The gun-blue swingle, heaving like a flail,
And hacks the coiling life out . . .

In those first three books the theme was *memento mori,* and their poems hurled a social and political indictment at decaying New England while they echoed the late-medieval, plague-haunted attitude toward death and decay. Corruption lay at the heart of the New England achievement: the capture of slaves, the slaughter of whales, the imposition of theocracy, and the lamentable deaths of ancestors. The early poems of Lowell circled obsessively around the presence of original sin but held out no hope for the bestowal of grace.

*The Mills of the Kavanaughs* is the most richly melodic, the most hieratic, the most New-England-haunted of all Lowell's work. The stylistic influence of Lowell's teacher John Crowe Ransom is more evident in this book. It is the least accessible and the least notorious of Lowell's books, and it contained (as had *Lord Weary*) a few "imitations," poems in which Lowell used a model from a foreign language to write a poem of his own that resembled, and in certain respects translated, the original. He has made dramatic versions of Racine's *Phèdre,* of stories by Hawthorne and Melville, of Aeschylus's *Prometheus Bound,* and he has since published a whole volume, *Imitations,* of lyrics and satires from numerous languages that he cannot himself read.

For some years after the appearance of *The Mills of the Kavanaughs,* Lowell appeared to be floundering in search of a new poetic style, having abandoned the rich textures that he had embroidered in his first two books:

. . . you trip and lance
Your finger at a crab. It strikes. You rub
It inch-meal to a bilge of shell. You dance
Child-crazy over tub and gunnel, grasping
Your pitchfork like a trident, poised to stab
The greasy eel-grass clasping and unclasping
The jellied iridescence of the crab.

This is preternatural writing, of the kind that the sea and its contents often seem to excite in Lowell: teeming, aggressive, chaotic, frenzied, gulping at violence for the taste of it.

Lowell's next phase was heavily, absorbedly, reminiscent. During the fifties he wrote poems about history, elegies to his friends, evocations of his family. In the last section of *Life Studies* (1959) he suddenly abandoned all rhetoric, all dogma, all evasion, all displacement of violence, and spoke as himself, naked, as in "Man and Wife":

> Tamed by *Miltown*, we lie on Mother's bed;
> the rising sun in war paint dyes us red;
> in broad daylight her gilded bed-posts shine . . .
> All night I've held your hand,
> as if you had
> a fourth time faced the kingdom of the mad—
> its hackneyed speech, its homicidal eye—

Or in the most famous poem in the book, "Skunk Hour":

> One dark night,
> my Tudor Ford climbed the hill's skull;
> I watched for love-cars. Lights turned down,
> they lay together, hull to hull,
> where the graveyard shelves on the town . . .
> My mind's not right . . .
>
> I myself am hell;
> nobody's here—

These poems were shocking in their confessional direct-ness, and they struck their first readers with terrific impact. As one of its reviewers, I must confess that my admiration for this book was at first outweighed by my discomfort. Viewed in the perspective of Lowell's total work, *Life Studies* now seems to me his highest achievement.

The synthesis of *Life Studies* was consolidated in *For the Union Dead* (1964), which contains some masterful pieces, like the majestic title poem, but also much that is trivial—fleeting and unresolved recollections of the past, friendships, love. The patrician begins to reassert himself. There is renewed talk of law, of the decadence of the present day. The magnificent title poem contains all these elements. The Boston monument to Robert Gould Shaw and his black Civil War troops has a Latin motto that says "He gave up everything to save the state." (Lowell, deliberately or not, alters it to say *They* gave up everything.) The poet calls on childhood memories of the South Boston Aquarium, where a teacher gave his class "an unhealthy, eager, little lecture on the sewage-consumption of the conger eel." The contrast is drawn once again between New England's tradition ("On a thousand small town New England greens, / the old white churches hold their air / of sparse, sincere rebellion"), its illusions (". . . Hiroshima boiling / over a Mosler Safe, the 'Rock of Ages' / that survived the blast") and its actuality:

> The Aquarium is gone. Everywhere,
> giant finned cars nose forward like fish;
> a savage servility
> slides by on grease.

This book, it seems, was Lowell's farewell to Boston. The title poem won the Boston Arts Festival Prize and was published in *The Atlantic Monthly* in November, 1959, just as Lowell was on his way out of town to New York. Once more it looked as though his autobiographical effort had left him beached. He was again to turn to a more generalized past and to prophesy on the American Experience, but there is more of the whale than the rainbow in his new work. In *Near the Ocean* (1967) he is gasping for air. Even in appearance it differs from his earlier books: it is bulkier, more expensive, decorated with uninspired drawings by the Australian artist Sidney Nolan, padded out to look grand. And it has returned to some of the themes of *Lord Weary's Castle* (. . . one more line / unravelling from the dark design / spun by God and Cotton Mather"). The book contains only seven original poems, none very long; the balance, 71 pages out of 128, are imitations, mainly from the Roman. Lowell has written better. The new poems reveal more clearly than his previous work the tug-of-war between the impulse to personal poetry on the one hand, and the

Imperial Style on the other. The Emperor has won out, the Napoleon who has so often served as a character in Lowell's poems.

The opening piece in *Near the Ocean*, "Waking Early Sunday Morning," was first printed in the *New York Review of Books* for August 5, 1965. In its original version, for almost the first time in his career, Lowell had in one poem brought the squalor and disappointment of personal life into collision with the horrendous impersonal forces in the world. For some reason, however, he thought better of this poem before including it in *Near the Ocean*, and in its 1967 version numerous lines have been deleted and substitutions made, not I fear for the better. The deleted lines are in italics.

> Oh to break loose like the chinook
> salmon jumping and falling back,
> nosing up to the impossible
> stone and bone-crushing waterfall . . .
>
> *Time to grub up and junk the year's*
> *output, a dead wood of dry verse:*
> *dim confessions, coy revelation,*
> *liftings, listless self-imitation,*
> *whole days when I could hardly speak,*
> *came pluming home unshaven, weak*
> *and willing to read anyone*
> *things done before and better done . . .*

Compare the two differing versions of the ninth stanza to see how Lowell here shrinks back from the personal into the grandiose, as he has seemed to do more and more often lately.

> Empty, irresolute, ashamed,
> when the sacred texts are named,
> I lie here on my bed apart,
> and when I look into my heart,
> I discover none of the great
> subjects: death, friendship, love and hate—
> only old china doorknobs, sad,
> slight useless things to calm the mad.

(1965)

When will we see Him face to face?
Each day, He shines through darker glass.
In this small town where everything
is known, I see His vanishing
emblems, His white spire and flag-
pole sticking out above the fog,
like old white china doorknobs, sad,
slight, useless things to calm the mad.

                                                        (1967)

Is not the second version the more elevated but the less poetic? Has not the author withdrawn himself and sent an understudy? Is not the new voice that of the custodian of culture rather than the poet? The 1965 version oscillates with increasing intensity between the public and the private dilemma, back and forth with perfect emotional rhythm, until the poem's great humming conclusion, identical in the second version:

peace to our children when they fall
in small war on the heels of small
war—until the end of time
to police the earth, a ghost
orbiting forever lost
in our monotonous sublime.

The 1965 version stretches the imagination taut between the private and the public agony until we can hardly bear it. The 1967 version, its stanzas' order chopped and changed, becomes a sermon on the inefficacy of religion to calm the savagery of our time. Lowell's self-revisions are among the most puzzling aspects of his work.

Would that I knew why this poem, and the others in *Near the Ocean*, should have been made so grim, cold, dutiful. As in his earlier work, Lowell locates the destructive element in the sea, in marine images of horror and fascination. Now, however, the terrible attraction of the swallowing sea becomes aligned with his Old Roman comparison between the Golden Age and the present corruption—as though, standing near the ocean, he were horribly compelled to plunge into New England waters and strike out hopelessly for the shores of the

*45*

Old World.[2] The personal style has faded away, the poetry of *imperium* has won its victory over the Virgin, and there is little left but resignation, for the Ocean has prevailed in its eternal battle against History.

> Sleep, sleep. The ocean, grinding stones,
> can only speak the present tense;
> nothing will age, nothing will last,
> or take corruption from the past.

∾

James Dickey began publishing poetry in 1957, and in an explosive ten years his work has developed in remarkable ways technically and imaginatively, yet all his poetry has dealt with the same central concern. The world is not for him a classical social structure based on a City governed by law, with a terrible ocean nibbling at its edges. For Dickey the world has depths and dimension that can be explored only by a sensibility that penetrates deeper and deeper beneath the guises of reality in the hope of finding a unity at the center. His poetry is, in the words of his poem "Buckdancer's Choice," "the thousand variations of one song." Unlike Lowell, whose work had matured in technique before he was thirty, Dickey, starting from scratch at thirty-four, brought a fully inhabited imagination to his work, but he had to find his own technique, a rhetoric that would enable his ideas and sensations to move freely in verse. It took him almost ten years to reach his full powers.

How was he to express his mystical intentions in concrete images? At the outset his poems sought elemental strength similar to the simple, gentle, poignant language of Edwin Muir. Lines like these, opening "The Heaven of Animals":

> Here they are. The soft eyes open.
> If they have lived in a wood
> It is a wood.
> If they have lived in plains
> It is grass rolling
> Under their feet forever . . .

---

[2] As Lowell would in life do in 1970.

bear a blood relation to the mysterious magnificence of Muir's "The Animals":

> They do not live in the world,
> Are not in time and space.
> From birth to death hurled
> No world do they have, not one
> To plant a foot upon,
> Were never in any place.

The similarity is more than stylistic. The older Scottish poet concerned himself with the same range of urgencies as Dickey: the "archaic companionship" of man and nature; the appearances of God in the world; the spirits of animals, trees, and water; the symbols of dream; the mysteries of flying and drowning in elements other than earth. Stylistically, Dickey's rhythms imitated Muir's in being unpretentious, conventional, deliberately unruffled; but there were more turbulent currents to trouble Dickey's underground river than Muir's still waters.

Dickey's work is a search, in a sense, for heaven on earth. He seeks order and resonance in the inchoate; ransacks through obsession, through trial and error, changes of costume and skin, through transformation of personality and the accidents of experience to discover some sort of relation between the human and animal worlds, a bridge between the flesh and the spirit, and, more than these, a link between the living and the dead. One source of this concern, frequently reiterated in *Into the Stone* (1960) and *Drowning with Others* (1962) emerges in reference to his dead brother.

> I look in myself for the being
> I was in a life before life . . .
>
> I cannot remember my brother;
>
> Before I was born he went from me
> Ablaze with the meaning of typhoid.

This brother is radiant with life in the poet's dreams and in his fantasies of companionship and resurrection. He is an alter ego who borrows the poet's body and connects the poet with the world outside.

Dickey's atavistic vision is like an echo, taking on shapes that shift into one another imperceptibly, unpredictably, mystically, as in "Inside the River":

> Break this. Step down.
> Follow your right
> Foot nakedly in
> To another body.
> Put on the river
> Like a fleeing coat,
> A garment of motion,
> Tremendous, immortal. . . .
>
> Live like the dead
> In their flying feeling.

Drowning and hunting are frequent images in the early poems. To drown is to become one with water, one with the dead. To drown in nature is to die on behalf of it, to enrich nature by losing yourself. Those who live are already the dying; only the dead therefore are spared the threat of extinction.

In his first two books Dickey had already established his poetic identity as a man restless within the confines of himself who must always be putting on other shapes (armor, helmets, hides, feathers, water) so as never to be only a single self, so as to become others, to rescue others. He remarks with amazement of sexual desire: "Someone lay with his body shaken / Free of the self." The ultimate ways of becoming more than the self are to copulate or die. Both unite us with others, with the animals, with the animal in ourselves; and the only way to understand the secret of death is to penetrate, to thrust, to cleave beyond the surfaces of nature to the ultimate kinship.

However, his technique still lagged at some distance behind his aspirations. He was handicapped as a poet by having come to his craft late, already knowing what he wanted to say but not how to say it. Most of the poems in the first two books, as also in *Helmets* (1964), leave the reader with the feeling that the poem has begun at the wrong place, or ended too late, after the reader's attention had already been used up.

Yet there are vibrant exceptions, like "Fence Wire," "Cherrylog Road," "The Scarred Girl," and "Drinking from a Helmet." In the last, several of Dickey's obsessive themes join forces. During World War II the poet stands in a line of soldiers waiting for water. He sees his face reflected in the water in a dead man's helmet: "I kept trembling forward through something / Just born of me." To see himself in another's helmet brings back once again Dickey's sense of substituting for his dead brother. "I knew / That I inherited one of the dead." The poem leads the poet backward in time, "into the wood / Until we were lost." Dickey had yet to discover a technique that would liberate him from his natural limitations— or else one that would take advantage of them. This poem, the last in *Helmets,* may have been a turning point. It brought him face to face with the memory of war, with the painfulness of the past remembered, and it embodied his theme in a narrative setting. He could no longer confine himself to sequences of images clustered around a central statement that would enable him to move backward and forward in time as well as in space, and he had to escape from the tyranny of the dactylic drone.

With *Buckdancer's Choice* (1965), Dickey began to break free and also to establish a reputation. He now opened up and exploited the possibilities of narrative—poetic narrative, not mere narrative in verse. Moreover, his liberation seemed to be accompanied by a liberation of violence, as though personal memories and poetic themes alike had long been suppressed. Now he began recovering for poetry his war experiences. Was it the memory of war, opened up almost twenty years afterward, that suggested new rhythms to him? Or was it the fighter pilot's memory of flying? Both themes hereafter made their presence more keenly felt than before. More urgent, too, is the reality of the past side by side with the present. A new metric, a new emphasis on narrative, the exploration of new themes and the extension of old ones, a freer use of the dimension of time—these four elements distinguish Dickey's maturity from his early work. In his themes of communion with the dead and the kinship of nature, he had established the possibility of a new voice in American poetry as audible as that of Theodore Roethke; but to attain it he would have to win through to the clarity of Roethke's vision and the resonance of Roethke's music.

The three major poems in *Buckdancer's Choice* are "The Firebombing," "The Fiend," and "Slave Quarters." All three have taken on narrative progression, and all three skip in great leaps backward and forward in time and space. A fourth narrative, "The Shark's Parlor," is a carnival of violence that falls short of success because the poet declines into his old habit of summing up at the end, in a moral that might have suited a poem of images but is out of place in a poem of narration. "The Firebombing" explores the relation between the corpulent householder of 1965 and the napalm-scattering pilot he was on a run over Japan twenty years earlier: "when those on earth / Die, there is not even sound . . ."

> It is this detachment,
> The honored aesthetic evil,
> The greatest sense of power in one's life,
> That must be shed in bars, or by whatever
> Means, by starvation
> Visions in well-stocked pantries . . .
>
> I swing
>
> Over    directly over the heart
> The *heart* of the fire . . .

"The Fiend," a dazzling performance, portrays a middle-aged Peeping Tom and his transcendent relationship with the women he peers at from trees and bushes at night. This poem is the first of more to follow that explore the realms of sexual aberrance.

> It will take years
> But at last he will shed his leaves    burn his roots    give up
> Invisibility    will step out    will make himself known to the one
> He cannot see loosen her blouse    take off luxuriously    with lips

Compressed against her mouth-stain   her dress   her stockings
Her magic underwear.

In these poems the mature technique makes itself manifest:
long lines with stresses far apart, emphatic pauses punctuated
by typographical spaces, frequent repetition of words and
rhythms, looping syntax. Sometimes the old dactylic cadence
appears, especially in short poems, but it is much altered in
the direction of subtlety.

The full power of Dickey's poetry becomes apparent in the
new-poem section of *Poems 1957–1967* (Wesleyan University
Press). The breakthrough surpassed even what might have
been expected.

> I have had my time   dressed up as something else,
> Have thrown time off my track by my disguise.

The rhythms are now remarkable indeed, and flexible as
acrobats:

> She was a living-in-the-city
> Country girl   who on her glazed porch broke off
> An icicle and bit through its blank bone: brought me
> Into another life   in the shining-skinned clapboard house
> Surrounded by a world where creatures could not stand,
> Where people broke hip after hip.
> ("False Youth: Two Seasons")

Dickey's oldest theme, that of man's reincarnation as angel,
returns in strange and novel form.

> I always had
> These wings   buried deep in my back:
> There is a wing-growing motion
> Half-alive in every creature.
> ("Reincarnation")

The theme emerges again in "Falling," a very long but not
really successful poem about a stewardess who falls from an

airliner and strips as she falls into eternity. In "The Sheep-Child" he investigates a theme as old as the Minotaur, sexual relations between man and beast, in terrifying eloquence:

> I saw for a blazing moment
> The great grassy world from both sides,
> Man and beast in the round of their need . . .

In "Sun," in "Power and Light," in "Adultery" ("me with my grim techniques. Or you who have sealed your womb / With a ring of convulsive rubber"), he deals with domestic relations and the love-hate between man and woman. In "Encounter in the Cage Country" he returns once again to the animals, but with a wolfish intensity that is new.

> the crowd
>
> Quailed from me    I was inside and out
> Of myself    and something was given a life-
> Mission to say to me hungrily over
>
> And over and over    *your moves are exactly right*
> *For a few things in this world: we know you*
> *When you come, Green Eyes, Green Eyes.*

All of Dickey's development, and all of his thematic complexity, are wrapped up in one long poem which opens *Poems 1959–1967*. "May Day Sermon to the Women of Gilmer County, Georgia, by a Woman Preacher Leaving the Baptist Church" contains everything that Dickey, at this stage, could put into a poem. The new metric and syntax were there; the obsessive theme of death and renewal and repetition and eternity; the transformations of the earth-bound; the archetypes of country life. It strains toward universality. Only time will tell whether it retains it; but this poem collects in one place everything James Dickey has been developing toward.

If American poetry needs a champion for the new generation, Dickey's power and ambition may supply the need. His archetypal concerns are universal to all languages and will no doubt carry over into translation; his sense of urgency is overwhelming; his volume, his range, his style, his technique, his process of maturing—all might supply W. H. Auden's five categories (and so might the number of bad poems Dickey has written!). There is no need for pessimism, yet there may continue to be a danger of overblowing. Such writing as Dickey's requires a vast fire to keep the caldron boiling. If he were to encounter a slight recession of energy, such as that which seems lately to have overtaken Robert Lowell, Dickey's value as a poet might easily enter into a decline just at the moment when his reputation, like Lowell's today, has reached its apogee.

# II

# Admirations

# The Last Word: In Remembrance of Alexander Pope

Alexander Pope dominated English poetry virtually from the publication of his first long poem, *An Essay in Criticism* (1711), until his death in 1744, shortly after the publication of *The Dunciad,* that all-out attack on pedantry and dullness. Pope, as a Roman Catholic who refused to sign an oath supporting the Church of England, was required by law to live no closer to the Court than ten miles. With his close friends Jonathan Swift and John Gay he formed the Scriblerus Club. *Gulliver's Travels, The Beggar's Opera,* and *The Dunciad* all began as "papers" for the Club, and all were aimed at political abuses of the time.

Less than five feet tall, hunchbacked, and gradually crippled by tuberculosis of the spine, Pope never married nor begot children, though otherwise he led a life of immense sociability and astonishing productivity. His *Works,* mostly in verse, run to ten volumes. His values were those of Western Christian culture as modified by the rediscovery of classical learning. If his translations of Homer affected for more than a century the way the English and their colonists regarded the epic quarrels of old Ilium, the scholars of Pope's time, like the brilliant and monstrous Richard Bentley, were sophisticated enough to challenge his taste. "Though it is a pretty poem, Mr. Pope," Bentley chided, "you must not call it Homer." To-day, with ancient Troy rendered more fittingly to our temper by Robert Fitzgerald and others, we might hardly recognize

*The Atlantic Monthly*, December, 1985.

our Homer in Pope's version, but we can certainly recognize our own species and its shortcomings in his rich, wise, and penetrating satires, the sort of poetry that no one in our century has been able to give us.

Endorsed by the received culture of his time, Pope could confidently take his seat as a taste-maker. Voltaire himself welcomed Pope's *Essay on Man* (1733) as "the most beautiful, the most useful, and the most sublime didactic poem ever written in any language." This majestic and slightly meretricious work set Pope on the intellectual throne of Europe. It seemed to approve the new science but hesitated at the door, for it could not help colliding with science's challenges to ancient authority. So long as the old values could be construed as tasteful, Pope might prevail, but it would become increasingly difficult to prove them true.

In Shakespeare the values of the Renaissance had manifested themselves as an explosiveness of invention, which could not have taken place at any other moment in the history of our language nor have been imagined without a theater where the verse could be spoken by living actors. Milton, half a century after Shakespeare, attempted to dominate English with such encrustations of allusion and metrics as to leave it an altered language, caparisoned with Christian humanism and nearly unrecognizable to, say, Chaucer. Pope's ambition lay closer within reach. Inheriting the "correct" and scrupulous diction of Dryden, he wanted to utter the last word on the classical age, and he desired that passionately enough to get his wish. Seldom has a poet so governed the taste of his era; seldom has a time been so willing to be governed.

Pope was born in 1688, the year when the Glorious Revolution installed a constitution and supplanted England's last Catholic monarch with a Protestant line. Those who, like Pope, opposed the new Whig notion of constitutional monarchy and yearned for a Catholic restoration were in danger of jail or exile but were soon neutralized by Sir Robert Walpole's parliamentary oligarchy. Despite this political settlement, the dominant English literary figures up to the French Revolution—Swift, Pope, Dr. Johnson—stood against it, espousing the Tory view based in part on ancient authority, in part on divine descent. Pope, though in opposition, dominated the literary culture of England throughout Walpole's hegemony—1721 to 1742. He spoke against the new government and in favor of order, decency, and taste.

What Pope said about these Tory virtues has often been remembered, even when we do not remember Pope as the author. "An honest man's the noblest work of God," "Hope springs eternal in the human breast," "A *little learning* is a dangerous thing," "For fools rush in where Angels fear to tread"—the list of famous lapidary lines could be extended. How often we find ourselves quoting Pope without knowing it: his words fill seventeen columns of the latest edition of *Bartlett's Familiar Quotations,* more space than is granted any other English poet save Shakespeare and Milton. By the mnemonic standard Pope cannot avoid being counted as one of the great poets of the past. He was dedicated to unforgettability: that was the point of his pointed lines. In writing of aging ladies of quality he claimed oblivion as the final indignity, elevating the unforgiving to the unforgettable.

> See how the World its Veterans rewards!
> A Youth of Frolics, an old Age of Cards,
> Fair to no purpose, artful to no end,
> Young without Lovers, old without a Friend,
> A Fop their Passion, but their Prize a Sot,
> Alive, ridiculous, and dead, forgot!

Maynard Mack's definitive biography[1] is the first complete life of Pope since 1900. It's the sort of book we rarely see now (975 pages, including 98 illustrations, 109 pages of notes, 44 pages of index). Among recent biographies it will, I imagine, stand with Irvin Ehrenpreis's three-volume *Swift* and Walter Jackson Bate's *Samuel Johnson.* Mack has clearly adopted Pope as his life work and has stuffed his book with every scrap of scholarship and wisdom that a long and thoughtful career could collect. His eye for history seems nearly perfect, even if

---

[1]Maynard Mack, *Alexander Pope: A Life* (New York: Yale University Press in association with Norton, 1985).

his ear for poetry strikes me as a trifle pedestrian, and the book exasperates by its sheer wordiness: no one would wish it longer.

Pope was the first millionaire—and perhaps the last—to earn his fortune as a serious poet. He manipulated the publishing machinery of his time, seeing to it that his letters were published during his lifetime but seemingly without his instigation, and that his poems of attack burst without warning upon his enemies, while his poems of friendship (of which there were a great many) were sedulously appreciated well in advance by those who loved him. He made a thousand enemies but foiled them by his skill. He engineered the publication of *An Essay on Man* to seem anonymous, so that his harshest critics would be tricked into praising it for its virtues instead of attacking it for its authorship. Mack describes him as "crippled, quick-tempered, highly sensitive to slights, at times vengeful, carrying out a career by sheer genius and relentless application in the face of envy, religious bigotry, and almost continuous slander." Perhaps in response to those slights, Pope's villa at Twickenham was constantly being renovated with grottoes and obelisks and busts, until it became as famous as he. During his lifetime at least sixty portraits of him were painted or sculpted.

Even Pope's peers and allies, when they displeased him, came under fire, as in the famous lines about Joseph Addison in Pope's masterpiece, "Epistle to Dr. Arbuthnot."

> Should such a man, too fond to rule alone,
> Bear, like the Turk, no brother near the throne,
> View him with scornful, yet with jealous eyes,
> And hate for arts that caus'd himself to rise;
> Damn with faint praise, assent with civil leer,
> And, without sneering, teach the rest to sneer;
> Willing to wound, and yet afraid to strike,
> Just hint a fault, and hesitate dislike . . .

On and on it goes, this anatomy of pettiness, an acidulously inked portrait of the literary lion.

Pope was not a poet, like most of ours, of introversion, of inner passions or self-inflation. His language, less elevated than that of the classical models he emulated, employed images of manufacture, of the human scale, of everyday understanding, above all of *control:*

> The spider's touch, how exquisitely fine!
> Feels at each thread, and lives along the line . . .

A Romantic poet might have attempted to *become* the spider; Pope made the spider seem almost human, a master spinner. Likewise with the famous lines, immortalized a second time by their musical setting in Handel's *Semele:*

> Where'er you walk, cool gales shall fan the glade;
> Trees, where you sit, shall crowd into a shade;
> Where'er you tread, the blushing flowers shall rise,
> And all things flourish where you turn your eyes.

How regulated poetry becomes when every gesture performed by nature takes on the style and scale of social understanding, when flowers *flourish,* gales *fan,* and trees *crowd,* all at the poet's summons—and when the original idea comes from a writer like Persius. This is the wild world as a landscape gardener conceives of it: this is civilization under control.

Any poet, whatever his era, would like to have been remembered as particularly as Pope. Since his time, relations between poet and audience have altered profoundly. Today's audience finds its poets unclear, irrelevant, unaccountable; our poets find their public dense, unresponsive, untrained to hear what we say. Poet and audience alike have a true grievance: poetry has taken a journey to the interior, no longer concerning itself with public matters, no longer able to invent, as Pope could, a diction that presumes public and private questions to be indistinguishable. Today what may the poet presume? That his reader shares the belief that poetry offers a way of living, a way of thinking and feeling, that stands in common to "all civilized mankind"? Far from it.

To defend such a belief against the assaults of a new mercantile society was Pope's ultimate commitment, for he and his friends-in-opposition saw civilization threatened by middle-class mediocrity, pedantry, and above all dullness. Putting on the armor of certitude, Pope wrote (and rewrote over many editions) *The Dunciad,* the ultimate eschatological Book of Revelation of the Age of Taste. It is at once his most magnificent sustained achievement and the poem most limited to the terms of his time. In the accents of Virgil he told the adventures of a hero of darkness, Tibbald (the misspelled name of one of his leading literary enemies), in his quest to found a great empire of dullness. Even now, in the Age of Efficiency, wireless, taped, and duped, we can respond to Pope's peroration, in which the whole world is set snoring and reverts to the beginning of things, when the earth was without form and void, and darkness was upon the face of the deep:

> More had she spoke, but yawn'd—All Nature nods:
> What Mortal can resist the Yawn of Gods? . . .
> Lost was the Nation's Sense, nor could be found,
> While the long solemn Unison went round:
> Wide, and more wide, it spread o'er all the realm;
> Ev'n Palinurus [Walpole] nodded at the Helm . . .
> In vain, in vain—the all-composing Hour
> Resistless falls: the Muse obeys the Pow'r . . .
> Thus at her felt approach, and secret might,
> *Art* after *Art* goes out, and all is Night.
> See skulking *Truth* to her old cavern fled,
> Mountains of Casuistry heap'd o'er her head! . . .
> Lo! thy great Empire, CHAOS! is restor'd;
> Light dies before thy uncreating word;
> Thy hand, great Anarch! lets the curtain fall,
> And universal Darkness covers all.

"A very pretty poem, Mr. Pope," says Maynard Mack, "but you must not call it prophecy." Perhaps not. Yet it is, and has remained, about the last word on mediocrity. And, as Pope said when rebuking the hapless poet laureate Colley Cibber:

> Poor Colly, thy Reas'ning is none of the strongest.
> For know, the last Word is the Word that lasts longest.

# "Quit Ye Like Men":
# The Maturing of Robert Frost

I can remember when Robert Frost came to visit my parents in Coral Gables, Florida. I was six years old and he was sixty. What impressed me most was his ankle-high black leather shoes. The date was early 1935. Such shoes even then were not common in Florida. But memory is stimulated by a photograph of five of us together, seated on a stone garden bench in front of the house where I lived that winter. My father is wearing a gunmetal blue suit (I remember the color, though the picture is in black and white) and white shoes, looking straight at the camera. My mother sits next to my father, wearing a knitted dress with a white coat over it, her hands self-consciously folded on her crossed knees, looking pleased to be included. Frost, in a light grey suit, a white shirt, no necktie, and wearing his redoubtable shoes, sits stolidly on the bench, both feet planted on the ground, like a man who had been through many picture-takings. My younger sister, hugging a large platinum-blonde doll, stands at the right end of the bench leaning against my father, while I, aged six, sit at the left end of the bench and the right hand of the master in short pants and droopy white socks, squinting into the sun. Why, when grownups took your picture, did they always make

Originally delivered in part as a lecture, which was published by The Library of Congress in connection with the centennial of Robert Frost's birth, 1974. Also published in part in the *New Republic*, March 30, 1974, under the title "The Self-Realization of Robert Frost, 1911–1912." Revised 1990.

you squint into the sun? We were in fact all squinting except Frost. When I look carefully I realize that his eyes are closed.

When this photograph was snapped Frost was still recovering from the death of his youngest daughter, Marjorie, who after giving birth to her first child had died of puerperal fever. Mrs. Frost had been suffering from severe angina and could not accompany him from Key West to Coral Gables. Frost stayed in my parents' house; during his visit my father apparently prevailed upon him to agree, during the following summer, to lecture to the students at the Writers' Conference in the Rocky Mountains, in Boulder, which my father would be directing.

In the lecture at the University of Miami, Frost would talk about poetry in the making. He said that poetry is provided by a combination of "things that happen to us and things that occur to us." He said that the best part of the poem is the part that never gets stated: "Its unsaid part is its best part."

A decade after the Coral Gables photograph, just after the opening of my Harvard freshman year in September 1945, when I was seventeen and he seventy-one, I met Frost again. My father had come to see me into college, and he took me to call on the old man at 35 Brewster Street in Cambridge, his grey mansard-roofed three-story house. Frost let us in through the tall frosted glass doors, where we were greeted by his border collie, Gilly, one of the two smartest dogs I have ever met.

My father and Frost had been acquainted ever since the 1920s, when my father immigrated to the United States from Britain, a vivid and enthusiastic poet not yet thirty. Frost quickly responded to the enthusiasm and encouraged my father to write a book about his life and work. Remembering his reception in Britain—before any poet practicing in America had even heard his name—Frost must have anticipated a second English appreciation. But the Yankee soon thought better of it when he learned that my father disliked Frost's friend and champion Louis Untermeyer, and he quietly told the publisher, John Farrar, then of Doubleday Doran, to turn to someone else. This story was never revealed in full in either man's lifetime, and I had heard no part of it before coming to the small living room in Cambridge in 1945. All this Harvard freshman knew of Frost was a pair of high black shoes, my father's admiration, a few anthology poems, and his fame. It would be another evening of literary talk, over my head no doubt.

Instead I found a wicked, entertaining, piratical old man with a strangely wrinkled face and a flickering, mischievous grin who sounded to me like the world's perfect ally against my father. My father took literature more seriously than religion; but here was Frost toying with the reputations of writers as cheerfully as a bull in a Wedgwood warehouse. He started out with Sir Walter Scott. My father had been pressing Scott's novels on me for years, and I had done my duty by them so far, nearly without pleasure. What a delight to hear Frost talking about how dull they were! how unreadable! how tedious, how stuffed, how stilted! And to see my father shifting uneasily in his chair, unwilling to contradict, as Frost, Scottish ancestry and all, attacked *The Heart of Midlothian* and left it for dead on the ground.

Subject No. 2 was "general education"—the 1945 term for the "core curriculum." I had already, after a week or two at Harvard, heard about little else. Frost had been an educational anarchist for forty years, and he was ready now to light into one of the foremost prophets of general education, the classicist John H. Finley, who was just commencing a course in conjunction with the comparative literature scholar Harry Levin called "The Epic and the Novel." "Once John has given the boys the Eliot House version of the *Odyssey*, Harry will want to give them the classical version of *Moby-Dick*," I remember Frost's saying. "I never liked *Moby-Dick* much," Frost confessed. "Too long. Too much about whale meat. I always preferred his little stories, the first ones, *Omoo* and *Typee*." As a boy who had never yet conquered more than the opening chapters of the Rockwell-Kent-illustrated edition of *Moby-Dick* that a kind family friend had given me for my birthday, I felt another thrill of delight. But more was coming.

The old man went on to ruminate on the way to read. He never, he said, put too much store in the virtue of finishing a book once you had started it. Why? Why even finish a chapter? The interesting thing about reading was what a book made you think about. He liked to stop reading as soon as a book gave him an idea to reflect on, to chew over. Teachers, Frost said, as my father's eyes remained fixed on the floor or the ceiling, couldn't help but think of books as *assignments*. He liked to think of them as ways of getting you to think, ways of getting you to quit studying, to go off on your own in quest of some sort of original idea, to become more yourself. What a gospel of good news! The young freshman, the good boy who had made his way into Harvard by slavish studying, could hardly believe his luck in meeting this old poet. How wonderful to be encouraged to quit, to run away from great expectations!

After this first conversation, I saw Frost two or three times a year for the rest of his life, an inestimable privilege. True, he was old and sometimes lonely for company, but he gave far more than he got in return. His conversation was wonderful, rhythmic, exploratory, wielding the American language as though he had invented it. His views on science and politics, on literature and teaching, on poetry and life, his reminiscences of the famous names in our century's roster of poets, combined to make me sleepless with excitement after each evening spent with him. But it was even more exciting to think of being encouraged into poetry by him. Once I started writing my own poems, in 1958, he asked to see them. No more, no less. Just to see them, he said, not to comment on them. And he never did comment, but he asked to see more, and without being prompted. (I was not canny enough to imagine why he never commented, not to me directly, though he did once mutter something like, "Too much of the sadness.")

During these years of course, Frost was becoming more famous than any American poet has been, in his own lifetime, before or since. Though he was born in 1874, the year Thomas Hardy published *Far from the Madding Crowd,* Frost survived well into the television age, and he made far better copy than Tennyson or Longfellow—or Hardy—would have. He had style. You could see into him, or so you thought. He looked a vivid picture with his slumped powerful body. His gravelly voice had character. When he recorded his poems—

and the "talks" that he seeded between them—on TV or on audio-tape, the atmosphere was—and is—magical.

Which of us has not dreamed about having to rise and give a speech—and going blank? Frost is one of those who has lived this nightmare, and at a presidential inauguration with four or five presidents, past, present, and future, sitting on the dais. It was a bright cold January day in 1961. The lectern from which Richard Cardinal Cushing of Boston was delivering the invocation caught on fire and had to be put out. Then the old poet rose up to read a poem he had written for the occasion. Maybe he knew it wasn't the best he could give and maybe he couldn't, as he claimed at the time, see the words in the snowy January glare, but he did substitute another poem, a better one. And then young President Kennedy arose to deliver his Inaugural address. It was, for better or worse, a day that changed all our lives, and the old poet was trying to claim a poet's share of the glory in the bad poem he never finished reading. The poem he fell back on, called "The Gift Outright," was, as we say now, something *else*.

> Something we were withholding made us weak
> Until we found out that it was ourselves
> We were withholding from our land of living,
> And forthwith found salvation in surrender.

Something else mishappened to Frost on that platform. Listening carefully to the recordings of the Inaugural proceedings makes it clear that *after* Frost read "The Gift Outright" he changed the last line in honor of the occasion, and recited it: "Such as she was, such as she would become, *has become, will become*." And then he went on: "and this poem—what I was leading up to was a dedication of the poem to the President-elect, Mr. John Finley."

John Finley? The classicist who wanted to make "general education" out of the *Odyssey* and *Moby-Dick?* The master of Eliot House at Harvard? Why? In 1938 there had been a move to make Robert Frost a professor at Harvard. His supporters had tried to place him in the classics department, since the English department, in love with T. S. Eliot, didn't seem to want him. It too proved reluctant. "I have scared myself with what I have set going," Frost wrote to one of his supporters in 1938. "It won't do for me to profess Latinity. I have been warned off already . . . with the suggestion that I might like John Finley as a watcher in my classes. Don't I know these bozos from old? They are too humanistic to be human."[1] What could Frost's deep memory have been doing to his thoughts on that January day in 1961?

John Finley was a handsome and charismatic figure, like the new president and certain other Harvard men. Finley had a certain look, a certain way of self-presentation that had more than a hint of the histrionic about it. Frost's official biographer, Lawrance Thompson, who warped Frost's malice into what amounted to a guiding principle, has misled many of us into going along with his judgment. Still, the scene will oblige the irreverent spectator. An old man who has a way of looking just like a Norman Rockwell grandfather obliges everyone's secret fantasies—both bad and good—by getting up at a presidential inauguration, rising in the cold, his hair fluttering in the wind, to recite the first poem ever uttered on such an occasion to the largest audience ever to witness such an event—and blowing it. Forgetting the words! And *then* — remembering them again! And finally, dedicating them to the wrong man. Who says poets do not fulfil the unconscious wishes of the people?

Robert Frost was far too secretive for any ordinary biographer, and the biographer he had chosen for himself, Lawrance Thompson, was, at best, quite ordinary, and, at worst, perhaps unbalanced. Yes, Frost was jealous, ambitious, manipulative, competitive, even two-faced, yet Thompson after more than twenty years on the job came to cherish every toenail on Frost's feet of clay. Thompson seems to have grown to hate Frost so cordially that he was simply unable to take account of Frost's more positive traits, and Frost, sensing this,

---

[1] Letter quoted in Lesley Lee Francis, " 'Imperfectly Academic': Robert Frost and Harvard," *Harvard Magazine,* March–April, 1984, p. 55.

approached at least one other writer with the plea, "I'm counting on you to save me from Larry." Three more recent books, Richard Poirier's *Robert Frost: The Work of Knowing,* William Pritchard's *Frost: A Literary Life Reconsidered,* and Stanley Burnshaw's *Robert Frost Himself,* have gone a long way toward redressing the balance. Was Frost vain? Of course. (As Evelyn Waugh wrote in *The Loved One* about an insignificant poet: "To the end he was the least vain of literary men and in consequence the least remembered.") Very few of our greatest writers have *not* been vain—George Herbert, Anton Chekhov, Elizabeth Bishop. What reason have we to expect any connection between human virtue and literary talent? Lives of great writers all remind us, *they* would not make their lives sublime.

After the death of Frost's father in San Francisco in 1885, Isabella Moodie Frost brought her husband's body east to be buried. Then she settled with her two children near his family, in Lawrence, Massachusetts, a mill town north of Boston not far from the New Hampshire border. Robert was eleven. He adored his mother and would do so always. At the time of the presidential inauguration in 1961 he used to say, "I wish my mother could see me now," not entirely as a joke. During his youth he slept in the same room with her, until at least the end of high school. The widow Frost had gone back to teaching school, earning a precarious living for her little family by teaching in various Massachusetts and New Hampshire towns, all within a ten-mile circle around Lawrence. When Robert graduated from Lawrence High School in 1892 he was already in love with his classmate Eleanor White, whom after a considerable psychic altercation he would marry in 1895. He had by then spent a year at Dartmouth College and dropped out to teach school in his mother's classroom. Once married, he went back to college for two years as a special student in classics and psychology at Charles W. Eliot's Harvard, but he had to withdraw in 1900 after the death in infancy of his eldest son (whose name as it happens was Elliott). He quit Harvard and went to live on a farm his father's father bought for him north of Boston. A year later his mother had died as well. The stage was set for one of the deepest clinical depressions in literary history.

Robert and Eleanor Frost spent the next ten years in self-imposed isolation on a farm near Derry, New Hampshire, where Frost struggled unavailingly with his poetry, with lack of money, with a sense of neglect, and with a growing brood of children whom he and his wife determined to educate on their own. These Derry years make up the darkest and most mysterious period in Frost's life. Letters from that time, and later statements about it uttered for the public, have a sound quite different from that of the Robert Frost we think we know. The letters of the Derry years sound aesthetic, eager to please, defensive, and genteel by turns. Frost's retrospective statements about this time carry the air of myth-making. His behavior among the locals of Derry was regarded as erratic, bad-tempered, hypersensitive, inappropriately proud. Still, up to this point in his life, say the age of thirty-five, he does not differ much from the youthful profile of other poets we have read about elsewhere: they too were voracious to learn, self-obsessed and self-conscious, diffident or rebellious or both in dealing with the world, touchy, moody, *depressed*. Especially for Frost and many other young men growing up in the late nineteenth century, *depressed* was the operative word.

We do not learn a great deal about Frost's inner life by looking at the evidence—it is rather sparse—of what went on during the Derry years, years devoted principally to family and to searching for a poetic voice. We do know that Frost wrote all or nearly all of the poems in *A Boy's Will* while he lived in Derry. I like to think of the Derry years, not in Frost's family life, perhaps, but in his poetic development, as a retarded maturation, as though a primitive creature were slowly awakening.

In the autumn of 1911 the Frost family had at last gathered the strength to "set forth for somewhere." They moved decisively for the first time since 1885 (except for an occasional trip or vacation) to a place outside the charmed circle of Lawrence and its surrounding towns, journeying north about one hundred miles to Plymouth, New Hampshire, near the White Mountains. Here, at Plymouth State College, Frost spent a year teaching women students the principles of psychology, and here too he lived in the town rather than in the country.

Those who had known him in the past were struck by the sudden alteration in him. As the biographer Thompson, churlish even when insightful, writes:

> This very touchy man of moods . . . had brought his arrogance and grouchiness under at least temporary control. At Plymouth, in his offhand conversations inside and outside the classroom, his remarks were usually cheerful, witty, mischievous, playful. . . . Even his speech was different from his talk at the time of the move from Lawrence to Derry in 1900. . . . Frost had gradually modified his way of talking. He deliberately imitated the manner in which his neighbors unconsciously slurred words, dropped endings, and clipped their sentences. By the time he reached Plymouth, glad to be rid of the farm, he was still perfecting the art of talking like a farmer.[2]

But *why* perfect such a way of talking, especially after living ten years on a farm and thinking it a trifle beneath him? Had he somehow in 1911 found a way not to withhold himself from the experience of his time and region? New England, sparse and barren, had been emptying out its farmland to westward migration for over a century. But for a poet might there not be something fertilizing about paying tribute to the New England sources of American strength? Might a poet, especially a poet who had been compelled to the task, get interested in exploring the fate of being condemned to farm barren land? Especially a poet in his apprentice phase, unrecognized and frustrated? Frost had already begun to accept the name and nature of farming, even though, as James Dickey has emphasized, he was clearly a lazy man physically when it came to real work.[3] But never lazy in writing about it. "The fact is the sweetest dream that labor knows. / My long scythe whispered and left the hay to make." Those lines had been written early in the Derry years. Now, in the fresh opportuni-

---

[2]Lawrance Thompson, *Robert Frost: The Early Years* (New York: Holt, Rinehart and Winston, 1966), pp. 370–71.
[3]James Dickey, *Babel to Byzantium: Poets and Poetry Now* (New York: Farrar, Straus and Giroux, 1968), p. 207.

ties and stimulations of Plymouth, his first college town and the first of many, Frost perhaps began to think more ardently about farming, rather than nature, as a subject for art, as Millet and van Gogh and others had done in the previous century: nature with man in the foreground.

However this inner decision was arrived at, by early 1912 it had taken effect. Frost wrote one of his editors, Susan Hayes Ward, before Christmas 1911 about "the long deferred forward movement *you* [my italics] are living in wait for," and he journeyed between terms to visit her in Newark, after sending her a new swatch of poems. He read on the train, as he went and came, a new translation of Henri Bergson's *Creative Evolution:*

> Our own consciousness is the consciousness of a certain living being, placed in a certain point in space; and though it does indeed move in the same direction as its principle, it is continually drawn the opposite way, obliged, though it goes forward, to look behind. The retrospective vision is . . . the natural function of the intellect and consequently of distinct consciousness.[4]

Now imagine Frost, returned from his journey to visit the only editor who had consistently encouraged his work and who had recently read and commended such poems as "Reluctance," "The Trial by Existence," and "October." Is it any wonder that his next letter to Miss Ward (January 15), not only asks her to remember "who it was that Luther thought the proper target to throw ink at by the bottleful" but encloses an early version of his frightening sonnet, "Design"? The following letter, written on February 10, 1912,[5] sounds remarkably like a dream, one of those dreams that, like Joseph's in the book of Genesis, alters everything. This letter holds in it phrase after phrase that students of Frost's work will recognize from some of his most central poems, many of them still far in

---

[4]Henri Bergson, *Creative Evolution,* trans. Arthur Mitchell (New York: Modern Library, 1944), p. 15.
[5]*Selected Letters of Robert Frost,* ed. Lawrance Thompson (New York: Holt, Rinehart and Winston, 1964), pp. 45–46.

the future, like "The Road Not Taken," "The Wood-Pile," "Directive," "Two Look at Two," "West-Running Brook," and "To Earthward."

> Two lonely cross-roads that themselves cross each other I have walked several times this winter without meeting or overtaking so much as a single person on foot or on runners. The practically unbroken conditions of both for several days after a snow or a blow proves that neither is much travelled. Judge then how surprised I was the other evening as I came down one to see a man, who to my own unfamiliar eyes and in the dusk looked for all the world like myself, coming down the other, his approach to the point where our paths must intersect being so timed that unless one of us pulled up we must inevitably collide. I felt as if I was going to meet my own image in a slanting mirror. Or say I felt as we slowly converged on the same point with the same noiseless yet laborious strides as if we were two images about to float together with the uncrossing of someone's eyes. I verily expected to take up or absorb this other self and feel the stronger by the addition for the three-mile journey home. But I didn't go forward to the touch. I stood still in wonderment and let him pass by; and that, too, with the fatal omission of not trying to find out by a comparison of lives and immediate and remote interests what could have brought us by crossing paths to the same point in the wilderness at the same moment of nightfall. Some purpose I doubt not, if we could but have made it out.

This dreamlike letter (signed "Nonsensically yours"), whose events strike its writer with "surprise," with "unfamiliarity," with "wonderment," shows the writer, in terms not unlike Keats's *negative capability,* involved in "the fatal omission of not trying to find out." To me the letter seems, in its compulsion, fateful. It signals the crystallizing of Robert Frost's talent at Plymouth, his having "set forth for somewhere."

> They are that that talks of going
> But never gets away; . . .
> I shall set out for somewhere,
> I shall make the reckless choice
> Some day when they are in voice

> And tossing so as to scare
> The white clouds over them on.
> I shall have less to say,
> But I shall be gone.[6]

In some portion of his soul he decided that his subject matter, at least for now, was to be the New England farmer and the farmer's wife and their discontents, and that the voice in which his poems would speak would be the farmer's own voice, the sound of speech, a new poetic, a new meeting-place in the crisscross forces of his life. *What could have brought us by crossing paths to the same point in the wilderness at the same moment of nightfall? Some purpose I doubt not, if we could but have made it out.*

If we can trust the dating of Frost's poems, the next one he wrote after the composition of the February 10 letter in 1912 was "The Wood-Pile," eventually published as the penultimate item in his 1914 volume, *North of Boston,* and possibly the first poem in that volume to be finished. Many regard it as one of Frost's greatest poems, and we know it is one he cherished, for in later years he sent his friends each year a new poem especially printed; and this, "The Wood-Pile," is the poem he sent out for Christmas in 1961, a year before his death.

> Out walking in the frozen swamp one gray day
> I paused and said, 'I will turn back from here.
> No, I will go on farther—and we shall see.'
> The hard snow held me, save where now and then
> One foot went through. The view was all in lines
> Straight up and down of tall slim trees
> Too much alike to mark or name a place by
> So as to say for certain I was here
> Or somewhere else: I was just far from home.
> A small bird flew before me. He was careful
> To put a tree between us when he lighted,
> And say no word to tell me who he was
> Who was so foolish as to think what *he* thought.

---

[6]"The Sound of the Trees," *The Complete Poems of Robert Frost* (New York: Henry Holt and Company, 1949), p. 195.

He thought that I was after him for a feather—
The white one in his tail; like one who takes
Everything said as personal to himself.
One flight out sideways would have undeceived him.
And then there was a pile of wood for which
I forgot him and let his little fear
Carry him off the way I might have gone
Without so much as wishing him good-night.
He went behind it to make his last stand.
It was a cord of maple, cut and split
And piled—and measured, four by four by eight.
And not another like it could I see.
No runner tracks in this year's snow looped near it.
And it was older sure than this year's cutting,
Or even last year's or the year's before.
The wood was gray and the bark warping off it
And the pile somewhat sunken. Clematis
Had wound strings round and round it like a bundle.
What held it though on one side was a tree
Still growing, and on one a stake and prop,
These latter about to fall. I thought that only
Someone who lived in turning to fresh tasks
Could so forget his handiwork on which
He spent himself, the labor of his ax,
And leave it there far from a useful fireplace
To warm the frozen swamp as best it could
With the slow smokeless burning of decay.[7]

One might scuff the radiance of this great poem to insist
too blatantly on ways in which it might be expressing aspects
of Frost's existential situation in February of 1912; but I think
I would also be remiss not to point out that the poem speaks
of being hemmed in by woods at twilight, of a bird who takes
everything said as personal to himself, though "one flight out
sideways would have undeceived him." It speaks too of find-
ing a kind of order hidden away in the depths of the woods in
that perfectly cut and measured cord of wood, "four by four
by eight," the only one to be found, a cord of wood tied up
with a cord of clematis, a cord of wood that bespeaks a legacy

---

[7]"The Wood-Pile," *Complete Poems*, pp. 126–27.

of human labor and human measure. A poem about trees, trees like those which, in "The Sound of Trees," had sounded over the house in Derry, trees "too much alike" to let the speaker know "whether I was here or somewhere else." When the bird hides from the walker he puts trees between them; and when the walker finds the woodpile, it is propped between one live tree and one dead one, like a body of work that is propped, Emerson-like, between the "courtly muses of Europe" and the live but frosty land of New England. I will leave it to readers to ask their own questions of this poem: I know it can stand the trial.

The rest of Robert Frost's early story is familiar enough to be summarized very quickly. Shortly after these inner events the Frosts decided to quit. They thought it a great adventure to make "the great leap forward." "Two weeks from the day of our decision, we were on our way out of Boston Harbor."[8] They sold the house in Derry and with the proceeds bought passage to England, sailing on August 23, 1912. In England they spent over two years living in this place and that, sometimes under thatch. In London Frost made the poet-friends whom he could never have met in Lawrence, Massachusetts: Yeats and Pound, Lascelles Abercrombie, Harold Monro, W. H. Davies, and Edward Thomas. By 1913 he had brought out in England his first book, *A Boy's Will*, poems written in his early youth and during the Derry years. In 1914 the English published *North of Boston*. Though the first book had caught the attention of the English literary avant-garde, it was his second book that saw Frost rise to new heights of originality with poems like "The Death of the Hired Man," "Mending Wall," "Home Burial," "After Apple-Picking," "A Servant to Servants"—and "The Wood-Pile." In the year that *North of Boston* was published in London, Frost turned forty. He had not yet published any book in his native country, yet once that deed was done he could return, as he did, triumphantly, in February 1915.

[8]Letter from Eleanor Frost to Margaret Lynch dated October 25, 1912, *Selected Letters*, p. 53.

Even as a small boy Robert Frost had dreamed about running away from home and being accepted by a race of noble savages.[9] The way a poet grows up as a poet is to find his own story and stick to it. An attentive reader could find twenty or thirty poems in which Frost tells in one form or another what he thought to be the story of his life: the story of a boy, or man, who runs away from civilization (San Francisco?), quitting for his own reasons, and goes off into the woods (New Hampshire) at the risk of getting lost, and finds there something worth taking note of, something that lies at the heart of the mystery. The most explicit and majestic of these poems, and the most mysterious, is "Directive," a poem Frost did not write till he was in his seventies, in which he instructs the reader,

> And if you're lost enough to find yourself
> By now, pull in your ladder road behind you
> And put a sign up CLOSED to all but me.

A similar story is to be found in that powerfully deceptive poem, "The Road Not Taken." It turns up in "The Oven Bird" and in "West-Running Brook," in "Kitty Hawk," and in many other places. In my visits with him Frost loved to tell about young people whom he had advised to drop out of school, to "quit ye like men," a phrase he quoted from St. Paul. His early and persistent fantasy of running away was most explicitly embodied in "The Bearer of Evil Tidings" (1936):

> The bearer of evil tidings,
> When he was halfway there,
> Remembered that evil tidings
> Were a dangerous thing to bear.
>
> So when he came to the parting
> Where one road led to the throne
> And one went off to the mountains
> And into the wild unknown,
>
> He took the one to the mountains . . .[10]

---

[9]Thompson, *Robert Frost: The Early Years,* p. xviii.
[10]*Complete Poems,* p. 416.

Though outspokenly rejecting escapism ("any who seek him seek in him the seeker"),[11] Frost in fact played the escape artist over and over again: from Dartmouth and Harvard, from Amherst and Michigan, from San Francisco to Lawrence, Massachusetts, and from St. Lawrence, New York, to the Great Dismal Swamp. In the last great journey of his life, which was first recounted in a touching little book by the poet and Russian scholar F. D. Reeve entitled *Robert Frost in Russia*, Frost ran away to the Soviet Union on an intercultural exchange and in a melodramatic, even a pathetic, journey reminiscent of Tolstoy's last terrible flight from his family, found himself alone in a room with Nikita Khrushchev, the Soviet party chief. He tried to speak to Khrushchev of magnanimity, of greatness, of grandeur. The American president, John Kennedy, was embarrassed by this episode, but Khrushchev felt differently. As Tolstoy's countryman, he said, "Robert Frost is a true poet."

In "The American Scholar," his 1837 Phi Beta Kappa Oration at Harvard College, Ralph Waldo Emerson said, "[Young men] do not yet see . . . that if the single man plant himself indomitably on his instincts, and there abide, the huge world will come round to him." Robert Frost had a lover's quarrel with Emerson, but the world came round to him. In the end, Randall Jarrell, that most resistant yet passionate of critics, would say of Frost: "One of the strangest and most characteristic, most dismaying and most gratifying, poems any poet has ever written is a poem called 'Directive.' " It is also the poem that most completely testifies to Frost's choice of escape, of vocation, of landscape, of heartland, which is why we as readers keep coming back to it, and to him. His instinct was always to set out for somewhere. "Directive," published when Frost was seventy-two, shows us the ultimate maturation of a poet, beyond which there is no room for further self-realization. The principal danger, once such a height has been reached, is descent toward the obvious, descent beyond John Kennedy to John Finley.

---

[11]"Escapist—Never," *In the Clearing* (New York: Holt, Rinehart and Winston, 1962), p. 27.

# Robert Frost: "I Want People to Understand Me—But I Want Them to Understand Me Wrong."

It's almost impossible now to hear an opinion of Robert Frost that doesn't begin by saying he was a nasty man. "[Stephen Spender] did not care for Robert Frost," wrote the late Margaret Manning in the August 26, 1984, *Boston Globe,* "but almost no one did." The novelist Harold Brodkey, who ought to know, wrote in the *New York Times Book Review* of August 29, 1982: "He was of a demonic vileness—I thought it showed in his face—a man devoid of moral judgment, as in his work, which consists mostly of morally blind statements, sly manipulations and shopkeepers' calendar apothegms." Even in his lifetime, friends expressed reservations. Archibald MacLeish, whom Frost ragged without mercy, wrote of "Robert whose smallness lived under his greatness like a crab under [a] palm." Bernard De Voto, at one time very close to Frost, later attacked him to his face: "You're a good poet, Robert, but you're a bad man."

Nobody claims, of course, that Frost was a public enemy, or that he committed a capital crime (like the treason that Ezra Pound was accused of), or that he fell into insanity like Robert Lowell or Delmore Schwartz, or that, like John Cheever or John Berryman or Elizabeth Bishop, he was a drunkard or a philanderer or even a homosexual. He showed nearly every symptom of the disease of ambition but never acted more obnoxious in its pursuit than did Sinclair Lewis or Ernest

---

Hemingway, and they won Nobel prizes. He exhibited no greater tendency to racism than many others of his generation; and, unlike most male writers, he wrote with great tenderness and compassion about the condition of women. His politics stood well to the left of Pound's and Eliot's and well to the right of the New Deal. The public loved him. What did he do to deserve posthumous damnation?

He may have been paying the usual price for becoming too well known before he died. The image he projected of a foxy grandpa on good terms with the establishment was not one to appeal to the iconoclasts of the 1960s. Frost struggled, after a very late start as a poet, to conceal his desperate need for recognition, and he could not conceal it completely. "All unusual energy," Bertrand Russell once wrote, "is inspired by an unusual degree of vanity."

But Robert Frost made one important mistake shared by no other major writer of his time: he tried to control his own biography. Frost was all too alert to the enemies he made, or invented, during his lifetime, for like many writers he suffered from more than a wisp of paranoia. For years Frost picked over biographers like apples in a barrel and finally settled on Lawrance Thompson, a Princeton lecturer and librarian. Thompson spent the last twenty-five years of Frost's life and all the rest of his own chafing at Frost's hide-and-seek ambivalence about being found out. Frost wouldn't have been an easy job for anyone, but in Thompson, whose *Robert Frost* was published in three volumes between 1966 and 1976, he had picked the wrong apple.

Thompson, a literal-minded scholar, crammed his work with invaluable information but never got over being shocked, even appalled, at the volcanic intensity of emotion he unearthed in the poet's inner life—the anarchy, the blazing anger, the fearful anticipation of insult. The stronger the emotion felt by Frost the man, the more Frost the poet tempered it in his work and found harmonious ways of expressing it. Yet the stronger Frost's emotion, the more it alarmed Thompson and the more Thompson distorted it for his readers. When an idea "occurred to" Frost, the biographer tried to nail it down like the flayed hide of an animal. When Frost betrayed jealousy or scorn, Thompson quailed and disapproved. When Frost evinced dislike, Thompson enlarged the emotion and spoke of Frost's "murderous thought . . . his killer instincts." The prose biographer could not forgive the poet for being a poet.

I knew Frost for eighteen years and saw him twenty or thirty times, usually over dinner at my house or after dinner at his. The acquaintance meant everything to me and, surely, not very much to him, but I learned more from him than from anyone else but my father. I never sat in his classroom, yet he was my great teacher, my *miglior fabbro*. Frost liked to say that the best part of a poem is the part not in words: "Its unsaid part is its best part." This was just as true of his conversation. There Frost was both ingratiating and unruly. He made you, his listener, feel that there was nothing to hide, nothing that he and you could not understand together as long as you could follow his way of putting it. His mind seemed to try on ideas like overcoats, dropping them on the floor when they didn't fit. Behind the search for a right fit lay his inner sureness of size and style, a sureness deftly yet hesitantly emerging. He always left me feeling uplifted, late at night after I had walked him home in Cambridge or Amherst and he had walked me back home, and I had walked him home again and, unwillingly, left him.

I was not alone in being encouraged to think of Frost as a friend: it was common to many who knew him no better than I did. The last president of Amherst College to deal with him, Calvin Plimpton, said in his 1963 eulogy, "There is almost no one who ever met him, however briefly, who does not claim him for his own." Frost always treated me as though I were an ally. The old man sat still, talking and talking, a mischievous grin playing over his strangely wrinkled face, his big hands, rough on the backs and smooth on the palms, making rhythmical chops in the air like someone splitting kindling with a hatchet, a gesture at once emphatic and lyrical, as though he were conducting his own music. At times like this, Frost was as good as any poet has ever been. You knew that you had been in the presence of a true poet, but also that the poet was your friend. We are always disturbed to find that our friends are only human.

Robert Frost asked for a lot: that perhaps the world might be slightly altered, and for the better, by poetry—by his poetry. In the end he was tricked by what he asked for, because he got it. He garnered more fame in his lifetime than any other American poet, fame amplified, moreover, by modern media. He also found himself misunderstood, and obtusely, by millions of readers because of those limpid surfaces in his poetry that help conceal the darkness and anxiety underneath. Most people see only the limpidity in Frost's poems, as they see only sweetness in the Mona Lisa. When Frost achieves inner seriousness with outer humor (as in "Provide, Provide"), most see only the humor and think him a buffoon. When he achieves inner humor with outer seriousness (as in "The Road Not Taken") most readers miss the irony and find him banal. Yet something in the interplay never allows them to forget what they have read. That is the unsaid part, the best part. That is the poetry.

Frost wanted not to be forgotten, but he also wanted not to be found out. He said to me once, "I want people to understand me—but I want them to understand me wrong."

He did not ask that one of his daughters should die after childbirth, two sons in infancy, another son commit suicide in his prime, nor that a granddaughter should be crippled by polio, nor that both a sister and a daughter should end their days in asylums for the insane. Even the most cordial Frost haters cannot blame him for all these happenings unless they are willing to credit him with enough charm to make trees fall in the forest. Frost's literal-minded friends have somehow constructed a posthumous version of his life that implicates him in every disaster and condemns his every success as the consequence of ambition.

"Forgive, O Lord, my little jokes on Thee / And I'll forgive Thy great big one on me," Frost wrote near the end, playing his own last joke. He underrated, however, the worst joke of all—the trick prose is able to play on poetry by taking the poetry out of it—and I doubt whether he would be willing to forgive that. In public he said he wanted to have written a few poems that would be hard to get rid of. He has certainly achieved that hope, but he also got his private wish. People have understood him wrong.

# Sylvia Plath 1: *Ariel*

Only rarely does a poet become the object of a cult. Sylvia Plath, age thirty, died in London in 1963, leaving behind her a sheaf of terrifying poems. Since then, and especially in the past year, poem after poem has been written to her memory by people who never knew her work while she was alive. The fable of "her abrupt, defiant death," as Robert Lowell puts it in his foreword to the American edition of *Ariel*, sees her as immolated on the altar of a cruel society, her poems the outraged byproduct of her last agony. But to oversimplify her life, making her into the James Dean of modern poetry, would also be to oversimplify and vulgarize the development of her work.

Sylvia Plath was a greatly but unevenly gifted woman who took the trouble, and had the intellectual resources, to train herself for a decade as a poet. Periodicals published a fair amount of her early work, written in her twenties, and it showed an unusual sense of rhythm, a vocabulary that had a long, accurate reach, and a protean talent kept under severe control.

The early poems, many of them published in a collection called *The Colossus* (first in London in 1961, then in a shortened version by Knopf in 1962), showed great promise but seemed, by comparison with *Ariel* at least, to have no absolute necessity for being. Many of them read like advanced exercises. She wrote a lot of prose as well, including a novel, but none that I have read so far seemed to me much out of the ordinary. Sylvia Plath's talent, though intensely cultivated, did

*The Atlantic Monthly,* August, 1966.

not bloom into genius until the last months of her life, when, if we may take the internal evidence of the poems in *Ariel* as our guide, she stood at the edge of the abyss of existence and looked, steadily, courageously, with holy curiosity, to the very bottom. The resultant poetry has a bone-chilling authority that could not have been achieved except by implacable attention. No artifice alone could have conjured up such effects; yet such is the paradox of art, these poems would never have come into being without the long, deliberate, technical training that had preceded them. We can only perform with true spontaneity what we have first learned to do by habit.

Every artist, and almost everyone else at one time or another, fetches up against the stark facts of life and death. No one can avert the gaze without some degree of self-betrayal. It has become fashionable—or if not fashionable, at least common—for poets to set down their autobiographical crises, first person and second person and all, as a qualifying confession to admit them to the fraternity—a kind of professional bad-conduct pass. All the difference in the world, however, lies between such antics, performed always with an audience in mind, and such terrifying lines as those that surface in *Ariel*. No matter whom the poems seem to address, they are written for nobody's ears except the writer's. They have a ritual ring, the inevitable preface to doom. From "Lady Lazarus":

> Dying
> Is an art, like everything else.
> I do it exceptionally well.
>
> I do it so it feels like hell.
> I do it so it feels real.
> I guess you could say I've a call . . .
>
> Herr God, Herr Lucifer
> Beware
> Beware.
>
> Out of the ash
> I rise with my red hair
> And I eat men like air.

From "Death & Co.":

> I do not stir.
> The frost makes a flower,
> The dew makes a star,
> The dead bell,
> The dead bell.
>
> Somebody's done for.

From "Elm":

> I know the bottom, she says. I know it with my great tap root:
> It is what you fear.
> I do not fear it: I have been there . . .
>
> I am inhabited by a cry.
> Nightly it flaps out
> Looking, with its hooks, for something to love.

To be given over to poems like these is to stand at the poet's side, frozen but powerless to reach a hand out as she falls. Though the poems have humor in them ("I guess you could say I've a call") it is gallows humor. Their hectic, breathless rhythms give plenty of evidence that they were written in dead earnest, as stays against confusion. What else is there to do when you are "inhabited by a cry"? Nothing to do but set down what you see, what strikes you, without compunction or consideration. That is what these poems have done. It is all poetry *can* do in the circumstances.

The poems in *Ariel* are poems of defeat except in one sense: that they exist at all. It would be preposterous to suggest that the experience embodied here is unique; but it would be a lie to suggest that experience alone could have written these poems, that they could have been composed by anyone but a true poet. They are a triumph for poetry, in fact, at the moment that they are a defeat for their author.

To have prepared, with all the devices and techniques of an art, for the awful catastrophe that you alone were fitted to face is to have sacrificed for art more victims than life can dispense with. One even infers from the grim joy of some of these poems that at the moment of writing, Sylvia Plath's life was consuming all its careful preparations. The candle is burnt out, and we have nothing but the flame.

# Sylvia Plath 2: *Crossing the Water*

We have only recently become accustomed—if anyone can become "accustomed"—to Sylvia Plath's Russian-roulette fascination with death as a healer, her dizzying conviction that attempted suicide could clear the head. Yet, as her newly published earlier poems seem to show, her vision did not clear till she had reached the very edge. She committed suicide in 1963, and it may always be impossible to read her work without the shadow of that knowledge.

Those harrowing poems in *Ariel* are thrust at us out of the ruins of her life. Since the poems themselves are obsessed with suicide, there seems no way to separate the poet's biography (even though it is not yet written) from her work (even though it is not yet all published).[1] The situation provides the perfect breeding ground for legend, for the cheapening of Plath's true and remarkable accomplishment, but her heirs, for whatever reason, have been publishing her posthumous work à la striptease, which helps the legend on its way. *Crossing the Water,* published late last year, contains some, but not all, of the still-unpublished poetry. These thirty-four poems were written, the jacket tells us, "in the transitional period between *The Colossus* (1960) and *Ariel*" (written in 1962 but not published till 1965). Another collection, *Winter Trees,* is promised, but there is no sign yet of a *Collected Poems. Crossing the Water* gives us at least some notion of the route she took from the

---

*The Atlantic Monthly,* February, 1972, under the title "Three Visionary Poets."

[1]No biography of Plath was published until 1976; no good biography until 1989. Plath's *Collected Poems* was not published until 1981.

highly accomplished exercises of her first work to the unmistakable genius of *Ariel.* Lines like these, from "Stillborn," look back to *The Colossus:*

> These poems do not live: it's a sad diagnosis.
> They grew their toes and fingers well enough,
> Their little foreheads bulged with concentration.
> If they missed out on walking about like people
> It wasn't for any lack of mother-love.
> . . . But they are dead, and their mother near dead with
>     distraction,
> And they stupidly stare, and do not speak of her.

The ear catches, as it is meant to, the studied effects of a phrase like "it's a sad diagnosis," or the flat ironic allusion to both pregnancy and idiocy in "bulged with concentration," but the poem as a whole seems to me quite ordinary, the lament of a literary lady clucking over the dryness of her work. Other expert, crowded, rather pointless poems sound even more frustrated, as though their author were trying to lift a stone while standing on it.

The poems in *Ariel* seem to be stimulated by some ghastly conviction that life can be bought only by the near presence of death, but *Crossing the Water* has not arrived at so advanced a position. Its poems teem strangely, however, with hospitals, nurses, stillbirths, operations: ". . . a terror / Of being wheeled off under crosses and a rain of pietàs" ("Apprehensions"). "The nauseous vault / Boomed with bad dreams and the Jovian voices of surgeons" ("Face Lift"). "Over one bed in the ward, a small blue light / Announces a new soul ("The Surgeon at 2 a.m."). Life is throughout the book threatened by lifelessness; birth is interlaced with death; the heart is menaced by the cold blindness of stone. "Love Letter" is typically scattered with stones throughout.

> Not easy to state the change you made.
> If I'm alive now, then I was dead,
> Though, like a stone, unbothered by it,
> Staying put according to habit . . .
> Now I resemble a sort of god

> Floating through the air in my soul-shift
> Pure as a pane of ice. It's a gift.

Not so much of a gift as all that, if you leap forward to "Lady Lazarus," one of the most heartbreaking poems in *Ariel,* and listen to how remarkably the tone has altered:

> Dying
> Is an art, like everything else.   [*Everything* else?]
> I do it exceptionally well.
>
> I do it so it feels like hell.
> I do it so it feels real.
> I guess you could say I've a call.

To return to *Crossing the Water:* only in a few poems—like "The Tour"—do we begin to encounter that acid contempt for the body, that carelessness about life itself, those clipped monosyllables, that scorching fury that can be overheard in the last recording of Sylvia Plath's voice. It was the voice of a woman obsessed by a vision:

> Toddle on home, and don't trip on the nurse!—
>
> She may be bald, she may have no eyes,
> But Auntie, she's awfully nice.
> She's pink, she's a born midwife—
> She can bring the dead to life
> With her wiggly fingers and for a very small fee.
> Well, I *hope* you've enjoyed it, auntie!
>
> Toddle on home to tea!²

---

²It would not be revealed until the publication of Plath's *Collected Poems* in 1981 that "The Tour" had been written five days before the recording, i.e., on October 25, 1962, at the height of the exaltation that produced the Ariel poems, and two days before the title poem itself. Nonetheless Sylvia Plath omitted "The Tour" from her planned contents for *Ariel.* Why? Because it might have caused pain to some person then living? *Bitter Fame: A Life of Sylvia Plath* by Anne Stevenson (1989) throws light on the reasons why some of Plath's most excoriating poems were not published in *Ariel* despite their author's initial intentions, but this poem falls into another category.

How frighteningly those "wiggly fingers" bring together the writer-typist and the nurse-midwife; and how that bald, blind, "awfully nice," inexpensive creature manages to embody the conflicting forces of life and death. Was Sylvia Plath in search of a larger vision that would include both?

*Crossing the Water* as a whole did not find it. The poems of this period disclose a world of stone and blazing light, inhabited by a whole population of these blind people. The poems repeatedly contrast the warmness of the heart with the coldness and blindness of the eye:

> O heart, such disorganization!
> The stars are flashing like terrible numerals.
> ABC, her eyelids say.
>
> ("An Appearance")

> . . . the scalding, red topography
> That will put her heart out like an only eye.
>
> ("Widow")

> I can stay awake all night, if need be—
> Cold as an eel, without eyelids.
>
> ("Zoo Keeper's Wife")

> When the soles of my feet grow cold,
> The blue eye of my turquoise will comfort me.
>
> ("Last Words")

> The trees of the mind are black. The light is blue.
> ("The Moon and the Yew Tree")

There are many more images connecting the eye that sees but cannot understand with the heart that beats but cannot feel. Childbirth and child-rearing seem to make no difference to this inner alienation; neither does love, not with a frozen heart. When the poems reach back through memory toward the poet's childhood, they still encounter the same parched and glittering landscape, the same abyss between the heart and the eye: "Stucco arches, the banked rocks sunning in rows, / Bald eyes or petrified eggs . . ." ("Whitsun").

*Ariel* would take Sylvia Plath up from this desert of death into the wild country at the edge of life. By then, exalted and exultant, she would no longer be separated from her vision, for the heart and the eye would have learned by some desperate stratagem to see as one:

> The blood jet is poetry,
> There is no stopping it.

The poetry in *Ariel* exudes an actual sense of relief in having drawn blood from stones, as though no price could have been too high to pay to irrigate the parched soil.

> The woman is perfected.
> Her dead
>
> Body wears the smile of accomplishment . . .

Yet the poet's irony never failed her, even at the end. The next lines of "Edge" read:

> The illusion of a Greek necessity
>
> Flows in the scrolls of her toga.

"The *illusion* of a Greek necessity." Her death was, like almost all suicides, unnecessary. It is reasonable to think that Plath might have agreed, had she survived her last "accident." There was no more *need* for her death to take place than there was a need for the visions in *Crossing the Water* to set her eye and her heart at loggerheads. It is both sentimental and ghoulish to applaud her self-sacrifice in "going all the way," for her death blithely brutalized a number of other people's lives; yet her dedication as an artist was as total as her humanity was defective. The moral enigma that colors her existence as a poet arises from the conflict between the two.

# Sylvia Plath 3: *Letters Home*

Sylvia Plath was above others of her time the poet of hate hissed between the teeth. In addition, she became a symbol of exploited womanhood, mostly because of her snide, cheap novel, *The Bell Jar,* which in these letters she repeatedly refers to as "a potboiler." *Letters Home,* a selection, with discriminating commentary by Aurelia Schober Plath, Sylvia's mother, from the letters she wrote to her family during her short life of thirty years, will give many readers of her poems a turn. Where is that scorn for hypocrisy that the dazzling poems in *Ariel* radiate? Where is that contempt for motherhood, success, convention?

The Sylvia Plath exposed in these letters is a gusher, a careerist, an ambitious scholarship student, continually counting coup in her battle for worldly achievement. The vast majority of these letters are written to her widowed mother, a brave and hardworking woman who, when Sylvia was eight, had to act as mother and breadwinner to two fortunately endowed children, necessarily force-fed on a diet of overachievement. The relation between the daughter and her mother (though not necessarily the reverse) seems to have been one of alliance in ambition. Sylvia Plath seems never to have learned how to recognize the bitch-goddess of success or to judge what price might have to be paid for a glimpse of that fanged smile. The posture of "letters home" is seldom the most graceful one for a child. Mother is not told the things that might worry her; nor does the child share the dark secrets of her personal and creative life. Only the shining surface of the moon is turned

*Boston Globe,* December 28, 1975.

toward the nurturing parent. Troubles are mostly glossed over or turned aside with deprecation. Successes, an *A* in a school course, a poem accepted by a magazine, an outpouring of work, the antics of a grandchild, are recounted with breathless pride. Only here and there does the rolling eye of danger show itself in a gleam of paranoia or overstrain.

These letters suggest that throughout her life Plath was exerting preternatural forces of self-control for her mother's sake; and that her mother has preserved these letters as precious testimony. It is a moving, saddening book, a chronicle of waste and unnecessary disaster. "Her physical energies had been depleted by illness, anxiety and overwork, and although she had for so long managed to be gallant and equal to the life-experience, some darker day than usual had temporarily made it seem impossible to continue." So Mrs. Plath accounts for Sylvia's final act of suicide. It is neither a glib nor a simple explanation.

*Letters Home,* aside from the light it throws upon Plath the woman, is full of unpublished poems and descriptions of her work as well: "Forget about the novel [*The Bell Jar*] and tell no one of it. It's a potboiler and just practice." "The medical profession has always intrigued me most of all, and the hospital and doctors and nurses are central in all my work."

Though for reasons of tact and perhaps libel these letters give signs of having been carefully pruned for publication (perhaps for the same reasons, there is no badly needed index), they stress the ties that bound Sylvia Plath to life. In the end such ties and great gifts could not prevail against the blindness, the surgically communicated hatred that chills such books as *Ariel* and *Crossing the Water.* How violently she seemed to be struggling, yet how little oxygen she left herself to breathe beneath that bell jar!

# Sylvia Plath 4: *The Journals*

Robert Frost used to advise young aspirants not to go into the arts unless they had "a snout for punishment." Sylvia Plath suffered, God knows, her share of punishment—some of it self-administered—but all the memoirs agree, and these journals bear it out, that she didn't have much of a snout. You could make a good case for a view of Plath's work as a poetry of incompleteness, of self-surgery, even, as Irvin Ehrenpreis has recently suggested, a poetry of the self as prosthesis, as a willful assemblage of ticktock inventory:

> First, are you our sort of person?
> Do you wear
> A glass eye, false teeth or a crutch,
> A brace or a hook,
> Rubber breasts or a rubber crotch,
>
> Stitches to show something's missing? No, no? Then
> How can we give you a thing?
>
> ("The Applicant")

To have known Sylvia Plath in her lifetime hardly helps me reconcile the selves looming out of her claustrophobic *Letters Home* and her self-lacerating *Journals*. These are as different as they could be from the gee-whiz braggadocio of *Letters Home;* these are the notes of a worker, busy as the bumblebees her father had labored to study. In Ted Hughes's short foreword he speaks of Plath's work habits as a process of nearly Islamic fanaticism, a wish to strip off everything to get at the

---

*Washington Post Book World*, April 18, 1982.

true self, though it was a self she masked in a hundred ways and which no one, not even Hughes, was ever completely shown, as he himself confides. Other witnesses who knew her well enough would bear him out. It may be that the quest in all of Plath's poetry was to discover two things: whether she herself was real; whether other people were.

The *Journals* give little evidence that she understood others. Plath's friends, even those closest to her, hardly ever receive a kind word in the journals, except when being useful or admiring. Sylvia's mother is praised for her maternal devotion—but then, in Sylvia's psychotherapy, poor Mrs. Plath is as deeply excoriated as the rest: I hate my mother in order to live free. This journal-keeper could hardly be more self-centered, mean-spirited, narrowly ambitious, envious of reputations like May Swenson's or (especially) Adrienne Rich's. Sometimes she speaks warmly of men, teachers and lovers, who enter her life as mentors and protectors. Ted Hughes himself is spoken of as titan, genius, emperor. She washes his feet, types his poems, irons his shirts, and does all that a girl can do to feel greater happiness for his successes than her own. But women? Women are competitors.

The real subject here (no headlines, no public events, no leakage from the real world) is writing, writing and success. Success was her true worship, a bitchier goddess than William James had imagined. To make herself a poet (which meant making herself complete) was one thing; but to make herself *successful* was the conscious aim. She had won every scholarship and contest, had been accepted by *Harper's* at twenty-one, by *The Atlantic Monthly* at twenty-three, by the *New Yorker* at twenty-five. Yet none of these ribands—and here is the *primum mobile* of horror in her work and her fate—sufficed to keep her from feeling like a *numb, blind, blank-eyed, stony, earthenware head,* all words and phrases that recur in her poetry with obsessive frequency. She must super-heat, like a welder, into completeness: "I catch up: each night, now, I must capture one taste, one touch, one vision from the ruck of the day's garbage. How all this life would vanish, evaporate, if I didn't clutch at it, cling to it, while I still remember some twinge of glory. . . . Hours of work. Who am I?" It is no wonder, perhaps, that when she sent the results of such efforts to Marianne Moore to get a fellow-ship recommendation, Miss Moore replied, " 'Don't be so grisly . . . you are too unrelenting,' and certain pointed remarks about 'typing being a bugbear.' "[1]

At other moments, detecting her own shortcomings in personal relations, Plath composed pathetic lists of how to improve her conduct, one of which concludes, "*Don't blab too much*—listen more; sympathize and 'understand' people." But mostly the journals are crammed with plans, plans for work, plans for prizes, plans for success, plans to be professional. The true vitality was reserved for her poems, but the *Journals* are full of what my late wife, Jane Truslow Davison, one of Sylvia's Smith classmates, described as "the dangerous illusion we shared, a belief in unlimited possibilities that was, I fear, closer to greed than to innocence."

Without dwelling on the posthumous publishing history of Sylvia Plath's works, I think the *Journals* can hardly be counted among the important literary items in the Plath catalogue, though their *biographical* significance, given their vacuous self-absorption, illuminates Plath's suspect ambitions for herself. Their writing style inadvertently repeats some of the major metaphor-chains in her poetry. But by any reasonable comparison with Plath's poetry, this is a depressing bore, scrapings of the last bits of dried flesh from the empty hide of the poet. She was, after all, an artist, not merely symbol of suffering and self-injurious womankind, nor the whipped egg-white that clarified the boiling broth of early feminism. How can we content ourself, then, with a book so riddled with editorial expurgations, with omissions that stud the text like angry scars, with allusions to destroyed and "disappeared" parts of the journals?

It reminds us of all the Plath biographies that got started but never finished, and of the one awful one that *was* published,[2] and of the nearly twenty years that passed after Plath's death before her *Collected Poems* were published in

---

[1]*The Journals of Sylvia Plath* (New York, Dial Press, 1982), p. 251.
[2]Edward Butscher, *Sylvia Plath: Method and Madness* (New York: Seabury Press, 1976).

1981. Wasn't there some deeply contradictory counterforce here, working as hard to cover up the poet's true accomplishment as Sylvia Plath did to dig her true self out of the sand? Does anyone imagine that Sylvia Plath herself, had she lived, would have permitted these journals to be set in type?[3]

---

[3]They still have not been published in England, only in the United States.

# Sylvia Plath 5: *Ariel Ascending*

Louise Bogan and Sylvia Plath emerged from New England a generation apart. Bogan, born in 1897, outlived Plath by seven years. Plath, born in 1932, took her own life in 1963 in London. Bogan in the 1920s in New York was grouped with such "Oh-God-the-Pain" poets as Sara Teasdale, Edna St. Vincent Millay, and Léonie Adams at a time when feminists were declaring independence. Plath was—perhaps unsuitably—claimed as a heroine by the liberationists of the 1960s. As a student Plath read Bogan's poetry and yearned to have her own work published in the *New Yorker,* where Bogan was poetry critic. Both women suffered emotional disturbance and spent time in mental hospitals, both bore children, suffered failed marriages, were uneasy lovers, and haters, of men.

Elizabeth Frank, in *Louise Bogan: A Portrait,* tells how Bogan grew up, daughter of a plodding white-collar worker and "a beautiful mother with an active, illicit erotic life." Mother sometimes took daughter along to trysts. Louise dropped out of Boston University at twenty to marry and bear a child after her brother was killed in the Great War. She wrote six volumes of poetry, plus reviews, stories, and translations. A second unhappy marriage to the *New Yorker*'s Raymond Holden, who could be described as a literary opportunist, led to more anguish, but she slowly recovered.

In her younger days Bogan had scarcely been able to control her rage, her "sneering," as she called it. She partly overcame it, compensating with fine-tuned lyrics that concealed more of her emotional life than they disclosed. In later years,

*USA Today,* March 1, 1985.

she followed a narrow routine, living in an uptown New York apartment that overlooked the mental hospital where she sometimes committed herself. Today her poems do not read well. They sound full of unstated agony, a little dreamy, a little dreary. In her lifetime, Bogan's reputation ranked high among poets but never with the public, though her *New Yorker* criticism was rightly admired. Frank's version of her life is sensitive, tactful and teacherly, but a little hard of hearing when it comes to the intonations of Bogan's poetry.

The fame of Sylvia Plath, *both* of whose parents, coincidentally, taught at Boston University, has far outstripped that of Bogan. Where Bogan spent creative energy to conceal her inner life, Plath labored unrelentingly to liberate hers. To the extent that her imagination sprang free, she ranks as a heroine indeed. The seventeen contributors to *Ariel Ascending: Writings about Sylvia Plath,* edited by Paul Alexander, explain the outcome of Plath's life more thoroughly than any narrative biography has to date. Those who have attempted to write her life have failed to stare her down, like workers trying to use an acetylene torch unmasked. Ted Hughes, her husband, writes: "All her poems are in a sense byproducts. Her real creation was that inner gestation and eventual birth of a new self-conquering self," as dangerous a quest as can be imagined, to herself and those around her. The writers, mainly poets, of *Ariel Ascending* create fascinating portraits. For anyone puzzled by the contradictory, disturbing genius of Plath, this is the book to read.

Plath holds a unique place in American poetry. To separate the creative from the destructive elements in her life and work is nearly impossible, so intimately do they interact; but the interaction lies at the bottom of what she achieved. Her poetic obsessions—blindness, coldness, scorn, death, and suicide— very likely were ways of healing herself and releasing her poetic gift. Her best book was *Ariel.* Ariel, in *The Tempest,* was a spirit who had been freed from a tree where a witch had entrapped him; but Ariel had to serve an indenture to the deposed Duke Prospero before liberation. Plath's spirit went free more than twenty years ago. Her Prospero, Hughes, was recently made poet laureate of England.

# Wallace Stevens

Stevens's work is less a poetry of emotion than a poetry of cognition: the servant not of the feelings but of the mind. His career had much the same quality. His undergraduate acquaintance at Harvard with Professor Santayana seems not only to have furnished Stevens with a model for philosophical poetry but to have provided an example for detachment in personal life.

Stevens's ultimate biography has not yet been written, but both his poems and his letters have some of the quality of self-hypnosis. He was "an ascetic by virtue of all his rejections and also by virtue of his devotion to the real," as he himself wrote about Courbet. His personal and his business lives were kept so separate from his poetic life as to constitute separate worlds; and in his early letters to his wife-to-be he wrote often about the creation of another world for the two of them: "I believe that with a bucket of sand and a wishing lamp I could create a world in half a second that would make this one look like a lump of mud."

Wallace Stevens, like his contemporary Robert Frost, was late in maturing; but unlike Frost he was deliberate about it. He was engaged for five years before his marriage, and his only child was begotten fifteen years after that when he was forty-four, after his first book, *Harmonium*, had been safely published. His early, somewhat timid ventures in the law bore little fruit until, at thirty-seven, he entered the insurance business, where he labored for the rest of his life, even for many

*Atlantic Brief Lives: A Biographical Companion to the Arts,* ed. Louis Kronenberger (Boston: Atlantic-Little, Brown, 1971).

years after he could have retired, living in Hartford and occasionally but with growing infrequency traveling south and west. Although his poetry is full of European tags and allusions, he never left the western hemisphere.

He was not at ease with himself as a young man. Between his boyhood in Reading, Pennsylvania, and his ultimate move to Hartford there stretches a mysterious and so far ill-documented era of lawyerly failure and poetic experiment in New York; but in those years he cautiously laid the base for his career, his marriage, and his poetry. His temperamental wariness seemed to suit the insurance business and enabled him to make a policy of his career and an accident of his life. Hence his leisurely development as a poet: he seemed unable to dedicate himself to the world of imagination until he had first mastered the procedures of the common world.

Like so many American writers, Stevens was haunted by the loss of his childhood, and the search for paradise and perfection in his poetry takes its psychic origins from Reading as surely as Mark Twain's quest for innocence leads to Hannibal. Stevens clung to his early vision out of a kind of duty, and perhaps that is what eventually leached it of overt emotion. Like Twain, he may have been alarmed by what he found when he got around to looking Home in the eye. After the publication of his first and finest work, *Harmonium,* in 1923, he ceased writing altogether for some seven years, whether out of discouragement, distraction, or despair of perfection. Then, at the age of fifty-two, he resumed, and the secret of his later poetic enterprise is embedded in the untiring fluency with which he composed for the rest of his life, repetitively seeking the changeless. Henceforward his private avocations as well as his poetic concerns would be arrangements: gardens, parks, zoos, views, music on records, paintings, *objets,* and books. The statement was always the same: "The Ultimate Poem is Abstract." "It is an illusion that we were ever alive."

Stevens's poetry is forbidding, fluent, elaborate, imperturbable, chaste, avuncular. "Having elected to regard poetry as a form of retreat," perhaps even as a form of worship, and having required himself to separate his factual life from his fictive life, he also shunned, as almost beneath the notice of poetry, certain varieties of resonance, conflict, and pain, and fixed his mind and talent exclusively on "the essential poem at the center of things." He was, in fact, an aesthetic puritan, endowing poetry with such high seriousness that the mere poet ("The demon that cannot be himself, / That tours to shift the shifting scene") can be regarded only as a figure of brittle comedy, as in "The Man with the Blue Guitar," or "Peter Quince at the Clavier," or "Le Monocle de Mon Oncle," or "The Comedian as the Letter C." His wit, with all its sense of manipulative play, is directed at man and at language, never at nature or illusion.

His obsession was of course with the relation of the mind to objects and events and thence with what he called poetry ("Poetry is the subject of the poem"). In pursuit of the Platonic vanishing point he developed an amazingly fluent, responsive, consistent, but at its worst, monotonous poetic style. Beneath its porcelain surfaces lies a sea in which the mind must sink and swim below the ceiling of the air. Perhaps its very self-containment, its airlessness, explains why Stevens's poetry has become a favorite subject for academic study. His images do not dominate his poetry, his poetry dominates its images, and the images serve him as talismans of the ultimate vision, no matter how often he asserts the opposite, as in the famous early lines:

> Beauty is momentary in the mind—
> The fitful tracing of a portal;
> But in the flesh it is immortal.

In practice Stevens turns increasingly to the abstract, and his language, while at best it incandesces in glimpses of subtlety and elegance ("Cuisine Bourgeoise," "Esthétique du Mal," and "The Rock," to name a few of the finest later poems), at worst passes into remoteness and sterility. Stevens is often, despite all the exotic gaudiness of his language, less evocative than he purposes. No other important poet of his generation utilized so seldom the dramatic opposition of characters and ideas, explored so infrequently the act of becoming, spoke with so single and cultivated and predictable a voice.

Stevens withheld from language—as in so many ways he withheld from his life—a full measure of vitality. The result is St. Elmo's fire in certain lines and verses; but how seldom we find in his work—and how often in the work of other major poets—a complete poem that moves through time and space like sculpture. He mouthed and chewed ceaselessly upon the real, without, it seems, often tasting it. His intelligence was enormous but obsessive, and after the dazzling achievement of *Harmonium* it spread out to encompass more and more examples of but a single idea, like a balloon that could grow forever larger without bursting. The later poetry is (the word keeps recurring) endless and endlessly evasive; to try to contain it is like trying to catch fog in a net.

The fairest evaluation of Stevens I know appears in an unerring poem of John Berryman's, a poet as unlike Stevens as it is possible to be:

> He lifted up, among the actuaries,
> A grandee crow. Ah ha & he crowed good.
> That funny money-man.
> Mutter we all must as well as we can.
> He mutter spiffy . . .
> What was it missing, then, at the man's heart
> so that he does not wound? It is our kind
> to wound, as well as utter
>
> a fact of happy world. That metaphysics
> he hefted up until we could not breathe
> the physics . . .
>             brilliant, he seethe;
> better than us; less wide.
>                       ("So Long? Stevens," Dream Song 219)

# "Deep in the Blackness of Woods": A Farewell to Robert Penn Warren

The town center of Stratton, Vermont, consists of four frame structures set in a high saddle among mountains, not one building dedicated to commerce: a town hall, a town office, a school, and an old, unsteepled, seldom-used church, all white, with no houses close by. Mourners were conducting last rites for an American writer on Columbus Day, 1989, in the hamlet of Stratton, Vermont, while the highways lower down were jammed with motorists gawking at flaming forests by way of celebrating the "discovery" of America.

The man his friends and family were burying was known as Red to everyone present, though his children and grandchildren called him Poppy. He had been born eighty-four years earlier, on April 24, 1905, just north of the Tennessee border in Guthrie, Kentucky, a town of about one thousand people given over to tobacco farming, chickens, kinfolk, and story-telling. His father, a bank officer, was a Warren; his mother, a Penn. Both grandfathers had fought in the Civil War. The family evenings in his Guthrie childhood could not have differed very much from those in Stratton, Vermont in his old age: low-lit rooms, dogs at the feet, a good fire, a glass of whiskey and a hearty dinner, woodland noises outdoors, and, inside, the sound of live voices telling stories, or reading them aloud, more often than not in a high, nasal, slurred Kentucky accent.

The stories the husband in Vermont read to his wife, who

*New England Monthly*, March, 1990.

could not see well enough to read, might be from the Bible, or the *Odyssey* or the *Aeneid*. In Guthrie the Bible had also been read, and the other stories had also told of slavery and its discontents, of scandal and conflict, of ribaldry and war, very much like those Warren would give his writing life to, in a body of work spanning forty volumes and six decades. The stories, recounted or invented, would involve a group of central themes: trust betrayed, the surprising darknesses of the human spirit, the illusions of history, the discovery of love through death, the softening of fate by affection, the hardening of love by fatality (*John Brown: The Making of a Martyr, The Ballad of Billie Potts, All the King's Men, Promises, The Legacy of the Civil War, A Place to Come To, New and Selected Poems, 1923–1985*).

Robert Penn Warren began as a poet, a student of John Crowe Ransom at Vanderbilt University in Nashville, and in his twenties was already identified with the "fugitive" poets who included Ransom, Donald Davidson, Merrill Moore, Allen Tate, and John Peale Bishop. Starting at about age thirty, with *Night Rider,* set in the Kentucky tobacco wars of the nineteenth century, he gave himself over to fiction, and at forty-one, even before publication of *All the King's Men* (1946), the portrait of a Southern demagogue, he moved to the North, never to live in the South again for any length of time. With his second marriage and the birth of his children in the 1950s, he began increasingly to give himself over to poetry, just as Thomas Hardy in England a half-century earlier had left novels in favor of poetry, marking the change with a huge epic poem. Hardy's was called *The Dynasts* (1903–8); Warren's, which he rewrote twice in later years, was called *Brother to Dragons* (1953), and it was the most ambitious attempt he ever made to get at the dark heart of the American dream. As he wrote in a 1979 preface: "Historical sense and poetic sense should not, in the end, be contradictory, for if poetry is the little myth we make, history is the big myth we live, and in our living, constantly remake."

From this time forward, Warren's life took its shape from New England. During the years he taught at Yale, lived in Connecticut, and summered in Vermont, his written work moved still deeper into poetry. In the last book he published in his lifetime, *A Robert Penn Warren Reader*, he listed thirty-eight books: sixteen books of poetry, eleven of fiction, ten of criticism, biography, history, and so on, not including such collaborative textbooks as *Understanding Poetry*, which educated an entire generation. Warren the poet moved gradually out of narrative poetry (though he never abandoned it) to lyrics and meditations, which filled the five volumes of poetry he published after his seventieth year.

These late poems combined his narrative instinct, his sense of the past, his feeling for landscape, with his remembrances of youth in such lyrics as those with which he ended *Audubon: A Vision* (1969):

> Tell me a story.
>
> In this century, and moment, of mania,
> Tell me a story.
>
> Make it a story of great distances, and starlight.
>
> The name of the story will be Time,
> But you must not pronounce its name.
>
> Tell me a story of deep delight.

Over and over again Warren's poetry would emanate from a speaker stunned with love for the mountainous landscape:

> Season late, day late, sun just down, and the sky
> Cold gunmetal but with a wash of live rose, and she,
> From water the color of sky except where
> Her motion has fractured it to shivering splinters of silver,
> Rises. Stands on the raw grass. Against
> The new-curdling night of spruces, nakedness
> Glimmers and, at bosom and flank, drips
> With fluent silver.
>
> ("Birth of Love")

> Deep in the blackness of wood, the tendons
> Of a massive oak-bough snap with the sound of a
> Pistol-shot . . .
>
> ("Reading Late at Night, Thermometer Falling")

Out of the peak's black angularity of shadow, riding
The last tumultuous avalanche of
Light above pines and the guttural gorge,
The hawk comes.

("Evening Hawk")

Vermont was the place where Robert Penn Warren, poet, became free to fly.

The mourners had come to the white church in Stratton less to marvel at the Himalayas of Warren's career (such celebrations would take place later on, in metropolitan and academic centers like New York and Nashville and New Haven) than to say goodbye to a friend in the place he had loved. They had come to recall a lean, muscular man, red-headed in his youth, a man of marvelous courtesy, broad wit, and snorting laughter, warm-hearted and hospitable, enormously yet inconspicuously erudite, athletic afoot and in the water, craggy in both body and features, who till the end of his days told stories in a thick Kentucky accent that few found easy to take in. (He used five syllables and more than the prescribed number of consonants to pronounce the word "literature.")

Those who loved Warren knew him not to be a religious man in the ordinary sense, but they also knew that a burial ceremony, even for a master writer, could not leap naked into newly invented language, as though death had never happened before. They resorted to one of the great literary texts of our language, transplanted from a mother country, the Standard Book of Common Prayer, its text unstained by postbellum adulterations. No minister would be necessary, for no sacrament was being administered.

One after another his friends and relatives arose, introduced by Warren's son Gabriel, and made their way, some haltingly, to the front of the church. Warren's biographer, Joseph Blotner, read the comfortable words; the music of Bach was played, exquisitely, by Carver Blanchard with a guitar and lute and Bill Crofut with a banjo; his oldest companions, some now wispy and faint of voice in advancing age, testified in turn to their friend's virtues and lamented his loss.

Cleanth Brooks, Warren's literary colleague of over fifty years, spoke of their scholarly and critical collaboration and praised his novels; Albert Erskine, his editor for forty years, described their chess competitions and how, as young men, they read together, the way young men will, the gloomiest poetry they could find; C. Vann Woodward, like Warren a profound student of the American South, bore true witness to Warren's lifelong dauntlessness as a swimmer; Saul Bellow spoke of his friend's candor, generosity, lack of pretense; a niece from Kentucky spoke of the glowing presence in her life and family of "Uncle Robert Penn." In between these reminiscences other friends read aloud poems by Thomas Hardy (nearer of kin to Warren's achievements in poetry and prose than any other writer in our language) and read or sang poems by Warren himself.

When the ceremony reached its end, the company made its way in caravan through a darkening afternoon along narrow back roads to a clearing in the woods a mile or two from the village center and, leaving their cars near the wall, walked up a knoll to an old graveyard, surrounded by oaks and maples, where the gravestones leaned, roughened with moss and lichen. The poet's four-year-old granddaughter Chiara was heard asking excitedly where Poppy's ashes were going to be buried. Here? Here? His widow, the writer Eleanor Clark, full of certitude and lean as the trees, stood with her handsome children, the sculptor Gabriel and the poet Rosanna, their spouses, and the three grandchildren (one newly born), at the heightened swell of the graveyard, and when all were finally gathered around the small excavation, Cleanth Brooks began reciting, in firm tones of resignation, the graveside words, "Man, that is born of woman, hath but a short time to live, and is full of misery. He cometh up and is cut down, like a flower; he fleeth as it were a shadow, and never continueth in one stay." The bearded poet John Hollander read one of Warren's early poems, "Bearded Oaks." Carver Blanchard stepped forward with his guitar and sang, softly on the chilly air, "Abide with Me," which had never sounded more beautiful than at this wooded graveside. When there was nothing left but silence, an attendant brought forward a pearl-grey marble urn of ashes to Eleanor Clark, who placed it in the cleft that had been prepared for it, and she and her children and grandchildren stepped forward in turn and took up handfuls of the cool moist earth to lay atop the urn. It was as though time were slowing down: one after another the mourners stepped forward, stooped, added a handful of earth to the vacancy, and walked slowly off across the coarse grass toward the road where their cars waited to take them out of the forest, while the day grew darker with the coming on of the clouds, and a few flakes of snow began to fall. Few could help stopping to look back at the place where their friend lay, a place they might, who knows, never see again, as the remaining mourners filed past the grave, stooped, let their handfuls of earth drop, and moved on, while beneath their hands the urn disappeared.

This was ski country, logging country, maple country. What was a boy from Guthrie, Kentucky, trained at Vanderbilt, the University of California, Yale, and a Rhodes Scholar at Oxford; a professor who had taught at Vanderbilt, Louisiana State University, the University of Minnesota, and finally at Yale; a writer who had written for nearly half his lifetime in Connecticut but also in Mussolini's Sicily, in postwar Liguria, in Brittany, Grenoble, and Grasse, who had travelled in Crete and Egypt, who had canoed in Canada and who in his late seventies viewed the terrain of the Nez Percé rebellion in Montana—what was this man doing seeking his eternal rest in Vermont? It was not the first time, after all, nor no doubt the last, that an American writer, deeply identified with another region of the continent, had sought final refuge in New England. Willa Cather, born in Winchester, Virginia, and raised in Nebraska, is buried next to a classic white church in Jaffrey, New Hampshire. Robert Lee Frost, born and raised in San Francisco but schooled in New Hampshire and Massachusetts, lies near Bennington, Vermont. Henry James, who was born in New York and died in London, reposes with his family in Cambridge, Massachusetts, overlooking the Charles River.

There may be something about the New England landscape that restores us to our notions of what America was and what it might become. Out of the decades that Robert Penn Warren and Eleanor Clark had been summering near Stratton came a desire to lie there after death. The plainness of the central tradition in American writing takes us back always, as Emerson (whom Warren cordially disliked) told us in *Nature,* to nature, to the thing itself, the stone, the leaf, the tree. When in his old age Warren poured forth a torrent of poetry out of a lifetime's weathering, his memory looked upstream to the limestone hills of Kentucky, yet he found himself speaking of the past from a veritable place in the present, in the words of the title of his last novel, speaking from "a place to come to." Just as the poems of Hardy's old age are embedded in the turn of a road, the shape of a hill, a pool in a falling stream, the street of a village, the echo of the choir in a church in Wessex, so the poems of Warren's last, and perhaps finest, period characteristically speak themselves in the tongue of a man standing on a ridge of the Green Mountains while the sun sets and a hawk soars overhead, a hawk like the one a boy shot at in the first story Warren ever published, in 1931.

In the final years of Robert Penn Warren's rich life he had come to rest here, in the land of white clapboards and maple syrup and covered bridges, in the midst of the mountains which the Bible so hopefully adored as the source of help, and which spoke to Warren in his age more eloquently than the hills of his youth. He saw the transition as the darkness of a covered bridge, in a poem of that title written near the end:

> Another land, another age, another self
> Before all had happened that has happened since
> And is now arranged on the shelf
> Of memory in a sequence that I call Myself.

And he concludes:

> What pike, highway, or path has led you from land to land,
>
> From year to year, to lie in what strange room,
> Where to prove identity you now lift up
> Your own hand—scarcely visible in that gloom.

Even in this rumination, written as he neared eighty, on the dark connections between youth and age, Red Warren could not help imagining his covered bridge as embodying a story, a "*sequence* that I call Myself." Why not accept burial where the darkness began to lighten, where the story ended rather than where it began?

# Stanley Kunitz at Eighty

Stanley Kunitz has been, symbolically, my teacher and model for nearly thirty years. During most of this time I have served as his editor and publisher. It has been a curious and rewarding interaction. I don't claim to be one of Stanley's intimates. I wish I were; the rhythms and claims of our lives have diverged too sharply. Business and geography have prevented us from meeting more often than once or twice a year.

I first became acquainted with him, notwithstanding, on the most intimate level in 1957 through his poems, when I read the manuscript of his *Selected Poems, 1928–1958,* which had been submitted to Emily Morison Beck, the associate editor of the Atlantic Monthly Press, at the suggestion of Richard Wilbur. I was then a puppy tugging at the leash of wanting to write, as I have written elsewhere, and my first conscious reaction to the stern rhythms of Kunitz's early poetry, while I sat reading it on a screened porch of my apartment in Cambridge, was one of distaste. I didn't exactly like the stuff: it bothered me. Those poems were not ingratiating in the 1950s manner. They were unfamiliar, disquieting, disturbing at a level I did not recall having visited. I put down the manuscript, walked indoors to pace around my third-floor study, and in time began to write what would be my first published poem: "I hear a child inside / Crying to be let out. . . ."

The Atlantic Monthly Press published *Selected Poems, 1928– 1958* in the year of its title, and it won rapt reviews from Robert Lowell ("He has never published an unfelt and unfin-

First published in a somewhat different form in *Worcester Review* 8, no. 2 (Fall 1985).

ished poem")[1] and Richard Wilbur and Marianne Moore and went on to win the Pulitzer Prize for Poetry. After his first thirty years in the wilderness Kunitz's name now began to resound in the places where it should long have been heard. He has never been among the most popular poets, but for those who have had ears to hear he has touched very deep, and the disturbance his work stirs up has sent out its ripples farther, year by year, poem by poem. Some of those only recently published in *Next-to-Last Things: New Poems and Essays* (1985) strike me as among the most numinous and penetrating he has ever written. He is, among twentieth-century poets, nearly unique (only Thomas Hardy and Robert Penn Warren can match him in English) in having been able to grow and change in old age and keep on changing in the depths of his own being. (" 'Live in the layers, / not in the litter' . . . I am not done with my changes" ("The Layers"). "It is necessary to go / through dark and deeper dark / and not to turn" ("The Testing-Tree").

Kunitz's output has moved at slightly faster than runic speed. Three poems a year for the last sixty, no more. Such minings in the earth cannot be hurried. Though he has traveled in recent years to Israel, Egypt, the Soviet Union, Eastern Europe, Britain, and to many parts of our own country as an embodiment of dedication to the art of poetry, and though he has touched the art of dozens of younger poets by his intimacy in reading and *listening* to the music of their apprenticeship, he has never needed to nourish their aspirations at the cost of neglecting his own. Like his admired Anna Akhmatova, like all great teachers in the arts, he has taught by example—and his example comprised patience, depth, care, uncompromising dedication to his art. He has known how to wait, and he has tried to teach others to wait, as in Simone Weil's sublime phrase, "*l'attente de Dieu*," words that combine in themselves the ambiguities of complete patience and complete attention.

In 1971, more than a decade after *Selected Poems,* Stanley

---

[1]Robert Lowell, *Collected Prose* (New York: Farrar, Straus and Giroux, 1987), p. 85.

came forward with *The Testing-Tree,* a hard-earned and richly deserved book, in which he hunkered down to an archaic simplicity of statement and to the bedrock of his own existence. In 1979 he put the last touches on the entire work of half a century, *The Poems of Stanley Kunitz, 1928–1978.* In between these mileposts, as the consequence of visits to the Soviet Union and a healthy collaboration with the late Max Hayward, he finished their bilingual version of *Poems of Akhmatova* (1973) and collected his fugitive essays in *A Kind of Order, A Kind of Folly* (1975). Throughout the years that I had a hand in publishing his books, while the Atlantic Monthly Press and Little, Brown watched him take on the patina of reputation, I marveled at the magical way he had grown in communing with the sources of his own work. To watch Kunitz fill with energy and "illuminate" while reading his own poems is to get as close to the sources of poetry as a listener is likely to.

Kunitz's work, about which much has been written, the best of it by younger admirers like Gregory Orr, Robert Hass, and Susan Mitchell, is not explicitly religious or, usually, heavily symbolic. Yet it seems to be attended by mysterious presences, by a nearly sacred aura. There are few poets left in our time who carry his bardic authority. To say one of his poems aloud, alone or with people listening, is to feel again the cold breath on the back of the neck, the sense of the real that only true poetry can bring us.

As Stanley Kunitz's "editor," who has never edited a line he wrote, I take hope from the example he has set: a poet in difficult harmony with his talent, a genius who finds resonances somewhere very deep in a mysteriously turning world. In 1977 he gave an interview that appeared in the *Paris Review* in 1982:

> The poem in the head is always perfect. Resistance starts when you try to convert it into language. Language itself is a kind of resistance to the pure flow of self. The solution is to become one's language. You cannot write a poem until you hit upon its rhythm. That rhythm not only belongs to the subject matter, it belongs to your interior world, and the moment they hook up there's a quantum leap of energy. You can ride on that

rhythm, it will carry you somewhere strange. The next morning you look at the page and wonder how it all happened. You have to triumph over all your diurnal glibness and cheapness and defensiveness.[2]

---

[2]From *Next-to-Last Things* (Boston: The Atlantic Monthly Press, 1985), p. 95.

# The Sandpiper Poetry
# of Elizabeth Bishop

When Elizabeth Bishop died in 1979 she was as highly re-
spected as any American poet living, though it must be said
that most of her champions had had a hard time explaining
themselves. In the praise they heaped on her one often hears
a stammer. "[Her] work is not easily labelled," wrote her col-
league Howard Moss. "She is not academic, beat, cooked,
raw, formal, informal, metrical, syllabic, or what have you.
She is a poet pure and simple who has perfect pitch." Robert
Lowell spoke of her in an overstretched metaphor: "When
we read her, we enter the classical serenity of a new country."
And even Randall Jarrell sounded vague when he said, "Miss
Bishop's poems . . . have a sound, a feel, a whole moral and
physical atmosphere different from anything else I have
known." When he wrote better, however, he came closer to
the crux: "In her best work restraint, calm, and proportion
are implicit in every detail of metre or organization or work-
manship." Even such praise tells us mainly that Bishop was
the kind of poet that these poets liked to think of themselves
as admiring. It is not, moreover, a simple task to describe her
special quality. Her publishers took the easy way out by call-
ing her simply "one of the master poets of the age." Now,
with the publication of *The Complete Poems: 1927–1979*, it
becomes possible, though not much easier, to isolate some of
the special qualities. Those who have read "The Fish" or
"Roosters" in an anthology somewhere deserve to have the

*The Atlantic Monthly,* May, 1983.

case made, and to look further into Elizabeth Bishop's enriching work.

Bishop's life, though not without heartbreak, would not seem at this stage of knowledge to throw more than fitful light on the poetry, and it has so far attracted little biographical publication. Will her biographer furnish us with revelations as garish as those disclosed by the recent chroniclers of Robert Lowell, Delmore Schwartz, or John Berryman? Born in Worcester, Massachusetts, and orphaned at an early age, Bishop spent part of her childhood in Nova Scotia and then attended Vassar College with "the Group," the gaudy generation adorned by Mary McCarthy, Eleanor Clark, Muriel Rukeyser, and other literary lionesses. She lived in Florida, Washington, New York, and, for many years, Brazil. During her last years she shifted between Maine and Boston, where she alternated with Robert Lowell and Robert Fitzgerald in teaching Harvard students about the writing of poetry. She was in person very agreeable, but not very brilliant, company—the sort of person it is possible to like very much without knowing exactly why. She bore herself with a sort of naughty gentility, like an unfrocked governess.

To seek explanations for why Miss Bishop's admirers stammer so, we must look scrupulously at her poetry and see how it repays the attention. She was visibly a poet of the open air, of *sky* and *sea*. These two words appear in a great many of her poems and balance one another again and again:

> The sun is blazing and the sky is blue.
> Umbrellas clothe the beach in every hue.
>
> ("Pink Dog")

> The water is a burning-glass
> Turned to the sun
> That blues and cools as the afternoon wears on . . .
>
> ("Pleasure Seas")

The poems often reflect reality in the way mirrors do—mirrors positioned in such a way as not to reflect the person of the viewer. This viewer remains very much out of sight, holding the mirror so as to bring the outdoors in. Even her earliest poem sparkles with reflections that leave the speaker aside:

> Her singing split the sky in two.
> The halves fell either side of me,
> And I stood straight, bright with moon-rings.
>
> ("Behind Stowe")

The poems also vibrate with color. Such words as "gold," "silver," "pale," "bright," "dark," "black," "white," "green," "blue," "red," make up the warp of her poetry. Few poets in this century can have been so mindful of color except Sylvia Plath, who steeped her emotions in felt color rather than in color observed and noted.

Still, the favorite play in Bishop's work is to mingle all the senses into one harmony, as in her poem "The Prodigal," where she portrays the prodigal son's experiences in eating husks with the swine:

> The brown enormous odor he lived by
> was too close, with its breathing and thick hair,
> for him to judge. The floor was rotten; the sty
> was plastered halfway up with glass-smooth dung.

If this can be called an indoor scene, it has in common what most of Bishop's interiors bring us: a sinister approach to buildings and cities, where her poems have a way of turning gloomy and breathless. Cityscapes affect her like an asthmatic attack: sometimes she struggles to breathe.

> At night the factories
> struggle awake,
> wretched uneasy buildings
> veined with pipes
> attempt their work.
>
> ("Varick Street")

The city, however, also arouses her sophistication and wit, as in the urban settings that burst out into the open air, like "Invitation to Miss Marianne Moore":

With dynasties of negative constructions
darkening and dying around you,
with grammar that suddenly turns and shines
like flocks of sandpipers flying . . .

One of her gifts is to transform light not into glare or fire or
even knowledge, but into peace and tenderness, as in "The
Shampoo":

The shooting stars in your black hair
in bright formation
are flocking where,
so straight, so soon?
—Come, let me wash it in this big tin basin,
battered and shiny like the moon.

Here as elsewhere, Bishop's poems are remarkable for the
calm sweetness of their tone. The sky in her poems acts like a
shelter, a comfort. Her landscapes behave with soft humanity.
One of them describes crisply, and better than any critic, the
nature of her own poetry:

solid but airy; fresh as if just finished
and taken off the frame.
("Brazil, January 1, 1502")

The world of Elizabeth Bishop's poetry, rarely harsh, seems to
avoid the preoccupations that we once thought of as mascu-
line only, and which crowd the work of her male contemporar-
ies: war, sport, overt ambition, violence, sexual aggressiveness.
Harshness in her poems is everywhere softened by the pres-
ence of sun, sky, clouds, moisture:

There are too many waterfalls here; the crowded streams
hurry too rapidly down to the sea,
and the pressure of so many clouds on the mountaintops
makes them spill over the sides in soft slow-motion,
turning to waterfalls under our very eyes.
("Questions of Travel")

No wonder she was so admired for the ways she differed from her male cohort. She made her name in 1946 with *North & South* and brightened it with *A Cold Spring* in 1955, when she won the Pulitzer Prize and woke every other poet up. It is nothing less than amusing to see how Lowell borrowed from her work in *For the Union Dead* (1964). Even so she did not hit her full stride until *Questions of Travel* (1965), her best book, in which her poems soften and mellow into a landscape that is permanently and unmistakably transformed into her own. What a wonderful tone "Arrival at Santos" takes! (See page 26.) It must be as ingratiating a poem as has opened any volume of American poetry since Robert Frost's *West-running Brook,* forty years earlier, opened with "Spring Pools."

Later on the energy in Bishop's work ran a little low, though many beautifully modulated poems came into being, like "The Moose" or "One Art" or the punningly entitled "The End of March." Many readers will relish the youthful poems, the witty occasional pieces, the glowing translations from the Portuguese, but I find myself remembering with most affection and impact the more mature, gentle yet acerb, pawky yet tender voice speaking of sea-margin and sky-margin, soft and cloudy, a little breathless, vivid with sound and color, in Bishop's master creation, an observant yet myopic "Sandpiper," reminding us of the sandpipers she associated with Marianne Moore.

> The roaring alongside he takes for granted . . .

> The world is a mist. And then the world is
> minute and vast and clear. The tide
> is higher or lower. He couldn't tell you which.
> His beak is focussed; he is preoccupied . . .

With what? Why, with the evidence of his senses, of course. His role in life, like his poet's function, is to tiptoe along the margin of things,

> looking for something, something, something.
> Poor bird, he is obsessed!

> The millions of grains are black, white, tan, and gray,
> mixed with quartz grains, rose, and amethyst.

Is there any other way to see eternity in a grain of sand except like this, through enunciating the very quality of seeing, halfway between sky and sea? The truest poet turns out to be the hardest to describe or praise for this very reason: she sees what others do not see. And then, through rhythmical recognition, summons up a quality of understanding that Kierkegaard characterized in the statement, "Purity of heart is to will one thing."

# The Saddest Englishman:
# Philip Larkin

Philip Larkin, perhaps the finest English poet of his genera-
tion, died in 1985 at the age of sixty-three, leaving behind him
a legion of frustrated admirers. This sardonic, lonely, despon-
dent artist was unique among the English poets after Auden
in his power to reach across national boundaries; but after he
first attracted American readers with his 1955 collection, *The
Less Deceived,* he eked out only two more collections in thirty
years, *The Whitsun Weddings* (1964) and *High Windows* (1974).
What Larkin's long-awaited *Collected Poems* reveals is that after
1974 poetry seems to have surrendered to despair and si-
lence: Anthony Thwaite has found fewer than twenty poems,
many unpublished, to speak for those last eleven years. But
this book does a tremendous service. Thwaite has carefully
arranged all of Larkin's mature poetry in order of its comple-
tion; and he has relegated youthful and apprentice work to an
appendix, which amply proves that nothing worthwhile has
been hidden from us. Thus the reader shares an almost bio-
graphical journey through the heartening rise and depressing
fall of a writing life. Born in 1922 in Coventry, Larkin showed
great precocity as a teenage poet, his muse vibrating to the
tunes of Auden. At Oxford, during the Second World War, he
was introduced to the work of Yeats by Vernon Watkins, and
he embraced Yeats in dozens of imitations. After Oxford Lar-
kin spent most of his mature life in the ancient but founder-
ing fishing port of Hull, in Yorkshire, where he served as

*The Atlantic Monthly,* November, 1966, and May, 1989.

university librarian and where he died. He was unusual among English poets in that he lived out his days in secondary cities, neither dallying in London nor spending any lengthy period of time in the countryside.

However despondent Larkin ultimately became, his poetry, in Thwaite's exemplary edition, reveals a youth that began in Wordsworthian gladness, in "a dream of sea and hay." Those increasingly rare poetic passages that deal with the satisfied senses seem always to evoke grass and the sea. But when Larkin's work ripened, after Oxford, he emerged as the most polished of craftsmen, the most inhibited of personalities, the most witty of self-deprecators. Yet Larkin discovered disappointment over and over again with an air of ghastly triumph.

> For you would hardly care
> That you were less deceived, out on that bed,
> Than he was, stumbling up the breathless stair
> To burst into fulfilment's desolate attic.
>
> ("Deceptions")

Once Larkin's Oxford phase was over, words like *failure* and *loss* began to steal into his poetry like recidivist thieves. Failure gradually wound its way, obsessively, into a desolate counterpoint to images of the sea and the fields. A classic instance is "As Bad as a Mile," Larkin's version of original sin:

> Watching the shied core
> Striking the basket, skidding across the floor,
> Shows less and less of luck, and more and more
>
> Of failure spreading back up the arm
> Earlier and earlier, the unraised hand calm,
> The apple unbitten in the palm.

The early work, expressing a time when meadow, grove, and stream called out to the poet, gradually gave way under the pain of some "obscure hurt" like that which afflicted Henry James and which, Larkin's poems intimate, arose from some sexual rebuff. A long poem, "The Dance," never finished, and published here for the first time, seems destined to get to the crux of the matter, but it breaks off in mid-sentence; other poems make mock of his frustrations:

> Sexual intercourse began
> In nineteen sixty-three
> (Which was rather late for me)—
> Between the end of the Chatterley ban
> And the Beatles' first LP.
>
> ("Annus Mirabilis")

In mid-career Larkin seems to have written with relative copiousness, though spurts of creativity alternated with periods of dormancy. At this stage his work increasingly declared its debt to the poems of Thomas Hardy: formal yet demotic, earthy, aware of society's discontents, ironic, though Larkin's work leans toward self-castigation where Hardy would have taken the road leading to grief and regret. Glimpses of the unfulfilled, distant love appear ("Leaving me desperate to pick out / Your hands, tiny in all that air, applauding") but are shoved aside by animadversions on the decline of England, whether in looking back to 1914 ("Never such innocence, / Never before or since," or, in "Homage to a Government," complaining that "Next year we shall be living in a country / That brought its soldiers home for lack of money") or expressing sardonic outrage at the state of the culture ("Don't read much now: . . . / . . . Get stewed: / Books are a load of crap"). Death becomes a second obsession, and age; in one poem, "The View," Larkin seems to be announcing his finish at fifty, even though at fifty Hardy, in his poetry, was just getting up steam.

At the bottom of this wonderful poet's imagination, however, lies the dominant late twentieth-century British vision, one of nostalgia for a glorious past (splendour in the grass) combined with a sour self-criticism:

> Truly, though our element is time,
> We are not suited to the long perspectives
> Open at each instant of our lives.
> They link us to our losses: worse,
> They show us what we have as it once was,

Blindingly undiminished, just as though
By acting differently we could have kept it so.
("Reference Back")

It is tragic to read through the exquisitely wrought, heart-breakingly endearing passages of Larkin's work and find the poet not only predicting his own failure but carrying it out, sinking from satire into obscenity, from self-pity into self-hatred, from disgust with society to withdrawal from it. Oh, the journey is illuminated with wit, as in "Administration":

Day by day your estimation clocks up
Who deserves a smile and who a frown
And girls you have to tell to pull their socks up
Are those whose pants you'd most like to pull down.

But the destination rings with pathos. One of Larkin's last published poems, "Aubade," begins, "I work all day and get half-drunk at night," and another commences: "I never remember holding a full drink." These late poems take on the mood of the aftermath of empire, nipping at the *chota peg* on the bungalow verandah while the native troops march back to their barracks, themes all too familiar from the fantasies, contemporary with Larkin, of "Masterpiece Theatre."

Perhaps this collective nostalgia has something to do with the reason why Larkin's *Collected Poems* sold 40,000 copies in England in its first six months—"Something to do with violence / A long way back, and wrong rewards, / And arrogant eternity" ("Love Again"). Larkin's poetry rings the knell on the white man's triumph, on the arts and riches of the island kingdom, on a culture of which he regarded himself as one of the last qualified, yet impotent, stewards, and it does so in the seemingly outworn music of rhyme.

English poetry since Larkin's heyday has turned to deeper, supranational roots in the primitive past, in the work of such poets as Geoffrey Hill and Ted Hughes, and only recently have such younger poets as Tony Harrison and Craig Raine, after a long grave pause to reflect, begun handling the instruments that Larkin left them—rhyme, humor, irony—to resume the sort of Little England music that this sweet, sad poet left us. To have this poignant collection of his work in one volume now is a great gift, one of the prizes of the decade.

# III

# Contemporaries

# A New Generation

With the disappearance from the scene, within the last several years, of almost all of the senior poets, an era has ended. Robert Frost, William Carlos Williams, E. E. Cummings, and Theodore Roethke have all died within the last eighteen months, and Robinson Jeffers and Wallace Stevens preceded them not by long. Ezra Pound and T. S. Eliot have all but stopped writing. Of all the important older poets only Conrad Aiken and Marianne Moore continue in possession of their powers. In the meantime, the poets who only a year ago were thought of as "younger" suddenly find themselves, in their forties, the makers whom still younger poets look up to: Robert Lowell, Richard Wilbur, Howard Nemerov, Robert Duncan.

Yet this sudden adjustment did of course not dawn the day before yesterday: it's been in the making for a decade. One sign of it has been the grouping of poets into "schools"—a symptom more of unrest than of binding alliances. Groupings of this kind help people sort themselves out but usually confuse matters more than not. A traveler who had been thought to be a member of one camp may quietly have packed his tent on his shoulders and wandered away according to his own impulse and need. The encampments are widespread and nomadic, and there are perhaps as many good American poets between the ages of twenty-five and fifty writing just now as there have been for a long while.

Like the poets of a generation ago—perhaps of any generation—the quest common to all of these younger poets in

*The Atlantic Monthly,* December, 1963.

search of a style is a rhetoric competent to register the full range of their feelings, yet one that will collect the inchoate into a clarity. A poet's style is more than an answer to a question; it is more than "the man himself." How does this tree, this grief, this sunlight embody itself in language—my language? If my language is inadequate to my experience, must certain realms of experience pass forever into darkness for me? This dilemma, as perhaps in the case of Conrad Aiken, sometimes works itself into the very stuff of poetry: the interchange between language and feeling, between sunlight and fog.

Robert Lowell has spoken of the distinction between "cooked" and "raw" poetry. Five years ago it was a just metaphor (I almost wrote "meataphor"), but the distinctions have already crumbled, as the best poets of the "raw" school have pushed farther out toward finding forms and styles for shaping experience, and the cooked poets have broken down the traditional forms of verse and diction to suit the voracious demands of what's around them. Edward Field, whose first volume, *Stand Up, Friend, with Me,* is this year's Lamont poetry selection, shows the growth of a meeting-ground for taste, for his book of fanciful, amusing, rueful, raw poems was chosen for its award by a committee of the cooked. Field has settled on one of the most challenging solutions to the dialectic between language and experience: utter simplicity. It lies as much in his rhythm as in his diction, and it makes him neither raw nor cooked but fresh. His verse runs in the "beat" mode in verse, but he has attained a distinctive rhythm:

> My happiness depends on an electric appliance
> And I do not mind giving it so much credit
> With life in this city being what it is
> Each person separated from friends
> By a tangle of subways and buses
> Yes my telephone is my joy
> It tells me that I am in the world and wanted
>
> ("The Telephone")

The flatness of speech is that of a telephone conversation between friends, yet Field gives it a turn, both for ironic humor and for pathos, that the language hasn't had recently. This raises the danger, of course, of playing the *faux naif*, but Field manages to avoid that by the natural sweetness of his feelings and by the sight of depth beneath his limpid surfaces. The three best poems in this book are as good as anything I have read lately: "Graffiti," a funny, romantic poem that unfortunately does not bear quoting in a family magazine; "Ode to Fidel Castro," a non-political sort of celebration in mock-heroic style; and "The Charmed Pool," which tells the story of a prince who, at a "charmed pool swarming with lower forms of life," kissed object after object, only to have them cast off their spells and become bores or disappointments:

> When a man tries the charmed pool and fails
> What can he do if he doesn't die of it?
> . . . Did he find the road back to where he came from?
> And learn like us to live from day to day
> Eating what's to eat and making love with what's available?

∽

The third volume by Brother Antoninus, *The Hazards of Holiness: Poems 1957–1960,* is a barbarous book of Christian endeavor, dominated by violence, and splendid despite its excesses. Brother Antoninus, previously known as William Everson, is a Dominican lay brother, older than Field, who has also been grouped with the Beats. Yet he brings to his poems a fierce Christian zeal, which makes his struggle with language emblematic of his spiritual wrestlings. He grabs for the first word at hand—if it rolls rhetorically enough. At other times he reaches clear across the table for the remotest words on the menu: ". . . he, the inveterate rapacity / Of the nerve's conquisitional itch; she, the indominate rigor / Of the martyr's faith . . ." ("Judith and Holofernes"). But at his best he possesses poetic fire to light his faith. He can recreate such moments of biblical confrontation as those of Jacob with the angel, Salome and John the Baptist, or "The Conversion of St. Paul":

> Crash!
> A brilliance so bright
> The noon blanked black

Overhead where the sun was;
Intense radiance unwombed;
One lasting clash,
One fast unfaceable spasm.

The horse uprearing
Outsprung from under,
Forked ears pronged
On the blinding intenseness,
The high-pawed hooves . . .

Crash!
The clang of fallen metal, armor
Rang on the road, the flailed scabbard,
That loose-sprung blade, grit-grating,
Steel on stone.

Such lines show Brother Antoninus at his best and worst. Words like "unfaceable," "unwombed," and "pronged" show how far he stretches the language beyond its refusal to give. But it is heartening to find a Christian poet who can bring such terrible passion to his writing, especially since Daniel Berrigan has proved disappointing after a rapturous beginning. Brother Antoninus reaches for the verb and finds his rhythms in incantation, with more substantial subject matter than some of his fellow San Franciscans.

At the cooked border of poetry the expansion of technique and subject matter have comparably altered. It may well turn out that the most influential recent volume of poetry was *Life Studies*, that strangely brilliant, disturbing testimony to a change of direction by Robert Lowell. Published in 1959, it brought, in its nakedness, its matter-of-fact autobiographical scruffiness, a dimension to the poetry of the East Coast that had been missing since Ezra Pound's work had as good as ceased, lying like a great city in ruins. Poets who, like Anne Sexton, W. D. Snodgrass, and Frederick Seidel, have taken the same bearings as Lowell, find themselves in a new, strange, unsettled country—"Between the unreal and the next world, stretched taut . . ."—where heightened perception is its own reward.

*Final Solutions,* by Frederick Seidel, complete with intentional echoes of Hitler and Eichmann, has in it the mutter of self-destruction, of self-immolation. These poems are sickening in their flirtation at the border between despair and madness. They are portraits, dramatic monologues, but they have about them the air of false diagnosis, in their use of such terms as "hebephrenic," "anosognosia," "pseudocyesis," "leukotome." They portray such characters as a woman psychoanalyst retired to live in Maine; an old Roman who dreams of a long-ago love and dies of a heart attack; a pregnant girl whose husband is dying of cancer; a young girl going mad. At times they remind one of the Hardy of *Satires of Circumstance,* but most often and most nearly they sound like Robert Lowell. The few fleeting moments of acceptance come with the experience of sensuality or else with a callow shrug of the shoulders:

> Convinced life is meaningless,
> I lack the courage of my conviction.
>
> ("After the Party")

This is self-conscious cookery indeed, as though the fury of Lowell's confessions were now to be put in the autoclave and made available for the clinic.

James Merrill's third book, *Water Street,* displays the work of a brilliantly visual poet, whose sensations come as from trick mirrors, prisms, colored glass, camera obscura, all the artifices of optics. His feelings, his views of himself are "illumined as in dreams." "Everything is cryptic, crystal-queer," freaked out in forty kaleidoscopic devices. Yet the visual Merrill is by no means deaf to sounds either in sensation or in the verse. In a poem about home movies he writes:

> My mother's lamp once out,
> I press a different switch:
> A field within the dim
> White screen ignites,
> Vibrating to the rapt
> Mechanical racket

Of a real noon field's
Crickets and gnats.

("Scenes of Childhood")

Merrill is a baffling poet. His glittering rhymes, the effortless subtleties of his free-verse poems, the play of sound against sense, all go to make up the repertoire of a gifted makeup artist. As he confesses,

Goodness, how tired one grows
Just looking through a prism:
Allegory, symbolism.
I've tried, Lord knows,

To keep from seeing double,
Blushed for whenever I did,
Prayed like a boy my cheek be hid
By manly stubble.

("To a Butterfly")

∽

May Swenson is one of the most ingenious and delightful poets writing today. In *To Mix with Time: New and Selected Poems*, she shows herself to have a wonderful eye for natural events. What does she not notice? A snake:

Mud-and-silver-licked, his length—a single spastic muscle—
slid over stones and twigs to a snuggle of roots, and hid.

("News from the Cabin")

Autumn:

Then hearse-horns

of macabre crows
sweep over; gibbet-masks
they cut on blue. I walk in husks,
in broken shafts of arrows.

("Executions")

A bird:

And a grackle, fat as burgundy,
gurgles on a limb.

>    His bottle-glossy feathers
>    shrug off the wind.
>
>                    ("Spring Uncovered")

A cat:

>    Not a hair
>    in the gap of his ear moves.
>    His clay gaze stays steady.
>
>                    ("Waiting for IT")

Her attention to detail gives May Swenson's poems a clarity of focus that is sometimes lacking when she turns in other directions. She needs, perhaps, the concreteness of things close at hand in order to see deeply: language in her hands tends to respond eagerly to the natural and palpable. She has staggering poetic equipment, visual acuity, a sense of form, a fine ear for rhythm and the colloquial. Among her recent poems too many attempt the shapes of arrows or zigzags or earthquakes, dealing with the Greater Scheme of Things. A series of travel poems—with the exception of one about a bullfight—strikes me as rather self-conscious, as though someone had been Taking Notes. Even though in her straining for fresh ways of saying things her sureness sometimes deserts her, yet she cannot go wrong with her nature poems. They are *seen;* the husks and kernels of nature are *there.* And sometimes, at moments of great simplicity, they go almost as far in eloquence as poems can, as in "Question":

>    Body my house
>    my horse my hound
>    what will I do
>    when you are fallen
>
>    Where will I sleep
>    How will I ride
>    What will I hunt
>
>    Where can I go
>    without my mount
>    all eager and quick

> How will I know
> in thicket ahead
> is danger or treasure
> when Body my good
> bright dog is dead . . .

A poem like this, in its lyric address, makes us forget all questions about the direction of poetry, about schools and generations. It is, after all, a song; and songs hold their own secrets. This one may hold the secret of long life.

# L. E. Sissman: "Did Shriner Die or Make It to New York?"

Sissman and I were nearly exact contemporaries: he was born six months ahead of me, on New Year's Day, 1928. We both came, as people say in New York, from Out of Town (I from Colorado, he from Detroit), and were schooled there. We were both half-Jewish, both attended Harvard, attempted New York, settled ultimately in Boston. From what he tells us of his life, he had a hothouse childhood and a precocious youth. Profiles seldom fail to mention his having been a Quiz Kid on national radio, and that, at thirteen, he won through to the National Spelling Bee in Washington, where, as he recalled later, he "bested some poor little girl from Kentucky on an easy word ('chrysanthemum' as I remember) and became the National Champion, the emolument of which office included a $500 Defense Bond, a wooden plaque with two bronze owls on it, and an all-expense-paid trip to New York."

The preciseness of observation is characteristic, but not what follows. "My main reaction to all this was to lose my lunch more frequently than usual, a long-standing symptom of my revulsion to performing in public, and to conceive a lifelong hatred for the exploitation of the young."[1]

Such remarks ought to lead us even farther back in time. Louis Edward Sissman was an only child, of parents who seem

---

Preface to *Hello, Darkness: The Collected Poems of L. E. Sissman* (Boston: Little, Brown and Company, 1978).

[1] L. E. Sissman, *Innocent Bystander: The Scene from the Seventies* (New York: Vanguard Press, 1975), p. 5.

to have been peripatetic, homiletic, and remote. His mother urged him to accomplish much. Like other gifted only children, he developed Interests—cars, planes, technologies, and varieties of expertise—that enabled a boy to go it alone under warily benign parental eyes. I am told that the elder Sissmans were specially alert, even perhaps cranky, about diet. When young Louis (as they called him) finally left home, bright boy, to go to Harvard, his filial letters would report faithfully on the wholesomeness of his food intake. The letters also requested, with preternatural insistence, money.

> My parents, who were constitutionally opposed to the idea of property, fearing its potential stranglehold on their freedom, never owned a house while we lived [in Detroit]. Instead, they rented run-down but commodious buildings which could house both my father's business and our living quarters. This neatly avoided the problem of living in the suburbs and at the same time put me in more than nodding touch with the heart of a city. . . . Still, I lacked more than the merest trace of a sense of belonging until, in 1944, I made the trip east to Boston."[2]

Though Sissman and I attended Harvard at the same time, and although our backgrounds, our interests, and even our friends overlapped, we never met there, nor for nearly twenty years afterward; and then our friendship, though it became more than professional, could not be described as intimate. I suspect that most of Sissman's friendships—with men at least—contained an element of soldierly standoffishness. Though much admired and beloved, though given to deep and explicit courtesy and capable of conferring a sense of warm camaraderie, he was not easy to get close to. His friends, therefore, seem to know very little about his life as a whole, but rather, each of them, about his or her part in it. His sense of personal privacy was acutely developed, yet it may have been linked to his artistic gift by a reverse mode, for his poetry, or at least that part of it written after 1963, had a very high autobiographical content.

---

[2]*Innocent Bystander,* p. 41.

Our knowledge of his earlier years, if we can clear a few openings unadorned by the foliage of his verse, might reveal a root-and-branch structure something like this: young, left-handed Lou Sissman arrives at Harvard in November of 1944, full-grown (six-four, two hundred pounds) but not yet seventeen. His assigned roommate is "a tall, courtly withdrawn youth who was so steeped in the Brahmin tradition that he sometimes seemed barely able to function in the real world."[3] He also welcomed the cheerfulness of the Irish maid assigned to clean his college rooms: "To me she was helpful, sensible, motherly, always forgiving: a kind of foster mother in my strange home, and one who never demanded the things my real mother did. . . . I never saw any reason to reconsider my vision of Boston as bound up in those two people."[4] Boston had set its seal upon his heart, and both his life and his work would be played out mostly against its background. Except for "a short, unhappy stint in New York," he would live in or near Boston till his death.

This sixteen-year-old freshman became a seventeen-year-old sophomore. Poems written in the 1960s testify to college escapades, observations and debauches, romantic pursuits of knowledge and honor. In 1946 the overstimulated eighteen-year-old was booted from Harvard, doubtless with good reason and probably with excellent effect. He got himself a job as a stack boy in the Boston Public Library, found a series of furnished rooms around Boston, and wrote home regular reports on his diet and health and regular requests for money, each request gravely particularized as to the benefits that would accrue. By the time Louis Edward Sissman was readmitted to Harvard in 1947, he was ready for more serious work. The furnished rooms had stirred up poetry. His teachers, John Ciardi, Andrews Wanning, and Theodore Morrison especially, commented encouragingly in the margins of "my dense, clotted, intentionally obscure verse of that period." His poetic technique set and was varnished: he received Harvard's Garrison Poetry Prize. On his graduation *cum laude* in 1949, a

---

[3]*Innocent Bystander*, pp. 43–44.
[4]Ibid.

year late, he was elected Class Poet. He had also married for the first time in 1948.

The chronological record now blurs a little. A fortune is sought, but not found, in New York. The National Spelling Bee Champion becomes for a while a copy editor at a now-defunct book publishing house but beats a somewhat ignominious and unemployed retreat to Boston in 1952. He takes odd jobs, some of them very odd, like selling vacuum cleaners. Eventually he lands in an advertising firm and likes it. He mingles with the motley population of the "wrong" side of Beacon Hill. But although this swathe of experience would emerge piecemeal in poetry written in later years, almost no poetry seems to have been written now, for perhaps a decade. Seen in hindsight his poetic silence is so curious as to be nearly as deafening as the seven-year silence that befell Wallace Stevens after *Harmonium*. Yet four significant changes occurred, more or less simultaneously.

Sissman mastered the craft of advertising and proved himself capable of making a good living at a business he succeeded and delighted in. He married for the second time in 1958, this time very happily. (There were no children of either marriage.) And at some stage (students and scholars may one day divine when, but I do not know) Louis Edward Sissman ceased being known as Lou Sissman, the home and college nickname, and became Ed Sissman, the business and literary nickname. Ed and Anne Sissman moved, after their marriage, to the country an hour west of Boston, significantly near the village of Harvard, Massachusetts.

Before the end of 1965 Sissman had compiled, in spite of a busy career, at least one typed volume of poetry. Some of it, true, had been revived from college notebooks. His newer work, however, dealt with the bone and marrow of his own past: Ed Sissman writing about the life of Lou Sissman, more than once in the poetry referring to himself as "Mr. Edwards." And then in the autumn of 1965 they discovered he had Hodgkin's disease, a disease that had once been "routinely fatal," but whose cure had by this time progressed far enough to give him an extra decade. Illness did not, except for intervals of hospitalization, radiation, and chemotherapy, stop or slow his output of poetry and, later, prose. For the rest of his life he wrote like one possessed of a knowledge remote from most of us, the knowledge of real time. His new poems only apparently resembled the thickly textured formalities of his undergraduate writing.

The 1950s, as some of us know firsthand, imposed certain terrible disciplines on people and on poetry. The early sixties, when Sissman began to write again, brought not only a new prosody and subject matter for poetry but publication of the breast-baring, bottle-draining confessional poetry of Robert Lowell, Anne Sexton, John Berryman. The year 1963 saw the deaths of Robert Frost, William Carlos Williams, Theodore Roethke, and Sylvia Plath. Poets were now expected to throw over the "constraints of closed forms," to question the past, to face down the Self. But approaches varied. Perhaps the reason Sissman and I were drawn together as author and publisher was that our work had certain resemblances. My own first book of poems, published in 1964, matched the work he was doing in private, insofar as it was written in rhyme, in blank verse, in stanzaic regularities. I have a clear memory of sighting my first Sissman poem, and of my reaction, probably in 1965, when "The Marschallin, Joy Street, July 3, 1949" was published in *Boston Magazine*. What a title! and what a strange, elongated, heavily epigraphed monologue this was, spoken by a woman named Mona Mountjoy, no longer young, watching the Cambridge Independence Day fireworks across the Charles River from her Beacon Hill bedroom window! What did lines like these have to do with the poetry deemed appropriate to the time?

> A small white integer appears,
> Bears a huge school of yellow pollywogs,
> And, with a white wink, vanishes.[5]

---

[5]From "The Marschallin, Joy Street, July 3, 1949," *Hello, Darkness: The Collected Poems of L. E. Sissman* (Boston: Little, Brown and Company, 1978), p. 55.

This portrait of a fading beauty dreaming of her past, her lovers, her town house, her city, her declining years, framed itself in a gold filigree of formal verse. It would take me a while, and it has taken the world longer, to get used to the sound of it. The poem was unsettling. Its deft way of speaking, both in the woman's voice and in the poet's, evoked a past that was neither sentimental nor tragic, neither frozen in ridicule, gasping in self-punishment, nor drenched in emotion. It was, as John Updike would later remark, "a middle tone."

By the time Sissman and I met at last, I had already read a number of his poems in the *New Yorker* and elsewhere. He turned out to be a long, slightly lopsided man, grave, formally dressed, extremely courteous, even owlish, so polite as to lend me confidence in my own opinions. Sissman's accumulated manuscripts proved that this pawky gentleman already had the makings of a book. Esther S. Yntema at the Atlantic Monthly Press helped me advise the author during 1966 and 1967 to winnow out his better (usually later) poems from his less good (and usually earlier). From his first volume, typed up before his 1965 illness on a large-lettered Underwood and entitled *Homage to Cambridge,* we ultimately selected only ten poems out of thirty-eight for book publication.

The first published book was entitled *Dying: An Introduction.* Such a title would of course prove a hard act to follow. While it was being prepared for publication not long after Ed's fortieth birthday on January 1, 1968, he continued writing not only poems but now book reviews for the *New Yorker,* in addition to his highly pressured advertising work. By now he was Creative Director for the Boston office of the advertising firm of Kenyon and Eckhart and would later hold a similar position with Quinn and Johnson. His first bout with Hodgkin's disease was over, but there would, as he could well imagine, be others, and he had much he wanted to write. After reaching that first grim awareness of the limitations of time, he began to write like what he was, an innocent man possessed. Possessed of a certain knowledge that things could not last, but possessed too of a wide-ranging engagement with the world around him—marriage, the advertising business, politics, hobbies, photography, old cars, new cars, food and drink, travel, but, above all, the life of words and their ability to make arrests. His work brought him prompt recognition of one sort: a Guggenheim Fellowship in 1968, an award from the National Institute of Arts and Letters in 1969, a cherished invitation to be Phi Beta Kappa Poet at Harvard in 1971. Some fellow poets praised his accomplishment, but those who dominated the poetry business of the time largely withheld their accolades.

Prior to his death in 1976, Sissman published three more books: *Scattered Returns* (1969), *Pursuit of Honor* (1971), and a book of essays selected from his five years of monthly *Atlantic* columns of the same name, *Innocent Bystander* (1975). After the end of 1974, to his chagrin, he was unable to write more poetry, though he continued to write successful prose until the last months of his life. Nearly all the poems published in the posthumous section of *Hello, Darkness* were written between 1970 and the cessation of poetic capability. The collected poems as a whole were written, with the few exceptions I have mentioned, in the dozen years between 1963 and 1974.

I have examined all the manuscripts I could find in his own files, or others, and decided, perhaps arbitrarily, that he would have wanted to collect mostly the poems from this period. Since he trusted me to edit his books when he was alive, I must believe that he would not have appointed me literary executor if he hadn't wanted me to exercise discretion in the selection as well as the arrangement. Most of the poems remaining from Ed's (Lou's) first, collegiate, "literary" career are in my opinion best left uncollected. If posterity thinks me wrong, posterity can seek them out at the Houghton Library, Harvard University, where they repose, and write a dissertation. I have also decided to exclude, with a couple of exceptions, the occasional pieces he dashed off on the typewriter or inscribed on the flyleaf of a book: such pieces were often private, though endearing, and he valued privacy.

In his life as in his work, Sissman was grave and formal, with a wry, ingratiating sense of humor. He never played the literary Brahmin in spite of his precocious learning. He dedicated his poem "Scattered Returns" to one "who knows how it is to be young and old."[6] He was a divided, complex man: business-man and poet, infant prodigy and late-bloomer, a slowly dying man trying to press the flowers of his youth between the pages of a book, a man as humorous as he was persistent, with the courage not only to be himself but to take himself with a certain wry modesty.

John Updike, to whom with Anne B. Sissman I am indebted for counsel and support in editing *Hello, Darkness,* has justly written of Sissman's poetry: "The metrical form becomes a shimmering skin of wordplay, compression, antic exactitude, sudden sweet directness, swoops and starts of rhythm. Though possessing the declarative virtues of prose—hospitable, even, to dialogue and narrative suspense—his poetry is always po-etic."[7] "Antic exactitude" says a great deal, an exactitude born of the obsession to recapture a past that might suddenly escape. It could, on the whole, be done to the life, only one day at a time, with poems specifically labeled as to place and date, and dedicated to those who might share the memory. But at least once, in "A War Requiem," Sissman, achieving his highest level of ambition and accomplishment at once, managed to evoke the historical forces that had dislocated an entire generation, his and mine. Born in the twenties, bred in the thirties, bewil-dered and polarized by the war, stunned by the evasions of the fifties, and coming of age, if ever, in the sixties, he concluded:

> I warm myself in isolation . . .
> I hide
> Out in my hideout from the memory
> Of our unlovely recent history . . .
> I see,
> By luck, a leisurely and murderous
> Shadow detach itself with a marine
> Grace from an apple tree. A snowy owl,
> Cinereous, nearly invisible,
> Planes down its glide path to surprise a vole.[8]

---

[6]*Hello, Darkness,* p. 95.
[7]John Updike, Introduction to *Innocent Bystander,* p. xvi.
[8]*Hello, Darkness,* pp. 147–48.

The poem is dated 1969, when New England saw not only a southward wave of snowy owls but signs that the Vietnam War would not quickly cease to be murderous. Standing by, as this sharp-eyed, worldly Innocent did with all senses open, he was not likely to be surprised by death, or murder, when it approached. In his last poems, some of them dreams or even nightmares, which he foresightedly entitled "Hello, Darkness," he watched the snowy owl as it, nearly invisibly, nearly inaudibly, planed down. And he might have grinned a little at the memory that the National Spelling Champion had been awarded a plaque with two bronze owls on it, and an all-expense-paid trip to the Big City.

# Space, Time, and Silence:
# Merwin, Strand, and Ammons

Confucius wrote, "Without knowing the force of words, it is impossible to know men." Perhaps the primary social use of poetry is to help restore the purity and the force of words—especially in periods of rapid social change, which nearly always have a vile short-term effect on language. In such times as these, slogans and jargon, especially abstractions suitable as fuel for idealism, leap into notoriety, then get dizzy and lose their way. For example, how revoltingly every interested party misuses "peace": the Soviets in Hungary, the Americans in Vietnam, the Weathermen in blowing up post offices. "The free world" includes any country that will take our money. "Law and order" in the 1970 congressional elections ceased even to be three distinct words: it contracted into "lawnorder," pronounced with an unholy suburban overtone reminiscent of Scott's Catalogue, as though skeptics were like crabgrass, to be mowed, poisoned, or edged out. "Racism" and "genocide," relatively new but useful words invented to describe systematic totalitarian policies of racial segregation and mass murder, have been blithely converted into the most casual of sidewalk imprecations. Yet in a few lines a poet can instantly reverse the contamination of propaganda:

> The best lack all conviction, while the worst
> Are full of passionate intensity.
>
> (Yeats)

---

*The Atlantic Monthly,* January, 1971, under the title "New Sounds, New Silences."

or:

> It is dangerous to read newspapers.
>
> Each time I hit a key
> on my electric typewriter,
> speaking of peaceful trees,
>
> another village explodes.
>
> (Margaret Atwood)

Poets have often herded us back toward simplicity. The sounds are new, but their silences are even newer; rests between the notes fall in unfamiliar places. Poetry, entering into the darkness of our emotional and spiritual lives, touches nerves and feeds hungers we didn't know we had, arouses senses so long neglected that we imagined them to be animal rather than human. Fashion pursues, it does not explore. It invents costumes and makes conversation. True innovation in poetry strips language naked. It has no fear of posing silence where fashion, self-conscious, would provide feverish chatter, amenities or clichés.

One of the new inventors of silence is W. S. Merwin, who after a series of four brilliantly turned books written in the manner of the 1950s, has in recent years sacrificed hypotaxis in favor of evocation and uncertainty. Milton:

> When I consider how my light is spent
>   Ere half my days, in this dark world and wide,
>   And that one talent which is death to hide
>   Lodged with me useless, though my soul more bent
> To serve therewith my Maker, and present
>   My true account, lest he returning chide:
>   "Doth God exact day-labor, light denied?"
>   I fondly ask . . .

In a comparable passage, written at forty-three (the same age at which Milton wrote his sonnet), Merwin leaves out a particular *kind* of material: the very signposts of time and probability that Milton exerted his resources of rhythm and gram-

*149*

mar to supply, to say nothing of (deliberately and skilfully)
omitting all punctuation, capitalization, rhyme, and meter:

> come out then
> the light is not yet
> divided
> it is a long way
> to the first
> anything
> come even so
> we will start
> bring your nights with you
>
> ("Beginning")

Time has all but vanished from Merwin's syntax, and while
this is his greatest strength, it also of course throws up a cor-
relative weakness. There are no words, like Milton's *when, ere,
though, lest,* and *fondly,* to guide the reader from present to
past, from actual to conditional, from declaration to evalua-
tion. But to omit those words is *difficult.* The technical re-
sources required to drop all that equipment are daunting in-
deed. Merwin has passed through a process of transformation
and self-instruction that, with a deeply serious end in view,
has left him with perhaps the most unerring ear and the most
formidable technique of his generation. He is a master of
sound as Picasso is a master of drawing, and he uses sound to
maneuver the rhythms of his poems so that their literal mean-
ing is unmistakable.

That does not make the ninety-two poems in his new collec-
tion "easy"—far from it.[1] As Merwin's title reveals, the man
who carries a ladder holds not only the rungs and sidepieces
but the spaces between them, and the ladder enables him to
use those very spaces to rise through space. Understanding
the silences is sometimes extremely difficult. These poems
inhabit an undifferentiated landscape and are written, even
more than most contemporary work, for the ear. They move
in the spasmodic rhythms of a speech that is groping for

---

[1] *The Carrier of Ladders: Poems* (New York: Atheneum, 1970).

pebbles in the dark and naming what its fingers feel. They almost require reading aloud to be understood.

> at the end
> birds lead something down to me
> it is silence
>
> they leave it with me
> in the dark
> it is from them
>
> that I am descended
>
> ("Kin")

Merwin's poems concern themselves with the divisions of reality (speech and silence, rungs and spaces, light and dark, solidity and emptiness) and aim to bring these divisions, these spaces within reality, under control in a unity of consciousness. When he faces this unity he can produce tiny poems that have the flavor of the finest *haiku:*

> Silent rivers
> fall toward us
> without explaining

or:

> Men
> until they enter that building
>
> ("Signs")

Poems like these are as concise and expressive as calligraphy. At the other end of the scale, a long poem, "Fear," is remarkable as Gerard Manley Hopkins's "The Leaden Echo and the Golden Echo" is remarkable—a tour de force.

Mark Strand, ten years younger than Merwin, would seem to have learned much from him, but Strand's tense, spare poems display a more explicitly moral and humane content than the cosmic spaces of Merwin's. His second collection, *Darker,*[2] con-

---

[2]*Darker* (New York: Atheneum, 1970).

tributes to a poetry of the self, by contrast with Merwin's poetry of existence. The poems carry an intimacy and a humor that makes them handy to quote in short passages:

> The rock is pleasure
> and it opens
> and we enter it
> as we enter ourselves
> each night
>
> ("Seven Poems")

The title comes from another short poem in the same sequence:

> I have a key
> and I open the door and walk in.
> It is dark and I walk in.
> It is darker and I walk in.

Some of Strand's best work echoes Christopher Smart, as in the witty poem that opens the collection, "The New Poetry Handbook":

> If a man publicly denounces poetry
> his shoes will fill with urine.

Or in two litanies:

> Let the great sow of state grow strong.
> Let those in office search under their clothes for the private
>   life,
> They will find nothing.

Most impressive of all is the closing section of the book, "My Life by Somebody Else," in which the speaker cannot imagine who it is who wrote those poems the world calls his.

If Merwin has mobilized the language to evoke our inner panics and vacancies, if Strand has undertaken to stalk the self in its cave, A. R. Ammons is more austere in his self-imposed limitations than either. Judging from his latest collection alone (*Uplands*, which is his seventh, and he is Merwin's age), Ammons moves as seriously in the exploration of spaces as Merwin does, but his curiosity isn't much piqued by the internal world of fantasies and distortions. *Uplands* does not deal often with people. Ammons manifestly and primarily dedicates his work to naming and ordering the external world, and the best of his poems engage words directly with the motions of natural process, devoting meticulous attention to the names of flowers and geological or biological phenomena, but always as poet rather than naturalist:

> knowledge is lovely
> but some of it shivers
> into the blood stream
> and undermines the
> requirements of the moment . . .
>
> ("Summer Session 1968")

Ammons's irony is rewarded with a breeziness of tone that, when his poems are working well and his words are falling into place, makes for a delicious equilibrium between speech and silence, between the understood and the unknown. His title suits his book perfectly: landscape, aspiration, and grammatical structure all echo the drama and motion of high country, mountains, and water, and in such a setting the poems can get swiftly down to their serious work of investigating the way the external world works:

> Up this high and far north
> it's shale and woodsless snow:
> small willows and alder brush
>
> mark out melt streams on the
> opposite slope and the wind talks
> as much as it can before freeze
>
> takes the gleeful, glimmering
> tongues away: whips and sticks
> will scream and screech then
>
> all winter over the deaf heights . . .
>
> ("Further On")

This is a poetry of process, of the passage of time, of how one appearance turns into another, of the relation between sensations and cognition, between experience and expectation. Such matters are not investigated without stretching the language, but how are we to locate the place where nature and man meet in language without stretching the point?

> and next if you're not careful
> you'll be
> arriving at ways
> water survives its motions.
>
> ("Classic")

Ammons combines modesty and confidence in rare proportions. They interact in patterns that excite his language into utterance that brings every muscle into play as it moves around in space and time.

# Visionaries: Kinnell and Wright

"If a man could pass through Paradise in a dream, and have a flower presented to him as a pledge that his soul had really been there, and if he found that flower in his hand when he woke—Ay!—and what then?" Coleridge asked. Keats, at about the same time, wrote of "Adam's Dream—he awoke to find it truth." Many of us are visionaries in the dictionary sense: we employ "apparitions, prophecies, or revelations." The private visions of poets set their unique aspirations at their unique obstacles: our poetry first erects the walls of our imprisonment and then contrives an avenue for escape.

Poets in this century are not favored, like Coleridge, with visions of damsels with dulcimers or of Venus rising from the sea; rather, we have tended to the apocalyptic. "The leaves were gray, as though chidden of God" (Hardy). "For Love has pitched his mansion in / The place of excrement" (Yeats). "I saw for a blazing moment / The great grassy world from both sides . . ." (James Dickey). "An old bitch gone in the teeth . . . a botched civilization" (Pound). These visions have been handed down by our poetic familiars, and we have become used to them. New poetry is often slower to move us: it takes time to accustom ourselves not only to a strange style of speaking but to an unfamiliar mode of envisioning our inner life. In his poetry James Wright is separated from his inner life by gravity: his body cannot aspire as his spirit does, and he envisions himself as a tree with fastened feet, or a bird, or an angel, engaged in a struggle to rise above mortality. Galway

*The Atlantic Monthly*, February, 1972, under the title "Three Visionary Poets."

Kinnell, more consciously in search of a single vision than some of his contemporaries, comes to possess not Coleridge's paradise but his "Nightmare Life-in-Death." The *agon* for both poets, born in 1927, is coming to terms somehow with what cannot be borne. Poets a decade or two younger, like James Tate or Diane Wakoski or William Matthews, have found a different style of suffering excrucation and move with greater nonchalance in the presence of the absurd.

Kinnell's *Book of Nightmares* is a single long poem of fourteen hundred lines that explicitly aspires to a single poetic vision. Its ten sections are interlinked in imagery. In this book, as in his earlier five, Kinnell writes like a man wandering by himself among mountains and cities, coming to himself outside society. His vision takes the form of a succession of related nightmares, each of which brings together images of the present and the absent, the living and the dead: the yearning to embrace a distant daughter or lover, the cadaver of a hen full of unlaid eggs, a pair of secondhand shoes that seem to guide the new wearer's feet, a hotel bed that sags under the weight of long-gone guests, a Vietnamese corpse that will not stop burning.

> I light
> a small fire in the rain.
>
> The black
> wood reddens, the deathwatches inside
> begin running out of time, I can see
> the dead, crossed limbs
> longing again for the universe . . .

Death and life interact over and over, both in the poem's imagery and in its skeletal structure. Unlike most contemporary imagery, Kinnell's is evenly balanced between indoors and outdoors, between the radiance of the sun and the gleam of the lamp. We can feel the muscles of the poem moving with the intensity of the poet's visionary preoccupations as he asks his question:

> a face materializes into your hands,
> on the absolute whiteness of pages

> a poem writes itself out: its title—the dream
> of all poems and the text
> of all loves—"Tenderness toward Existence."
> . . . Can it ever be true—
> all bodies, one body, one light
> made of everyone's darkness together?

and as he answers it:

> . . . I find myself alive
> in the whorled
> archway of the fingerprint of all things.
> skeleton groaning,
> blood-strings wailing the wall of all things.

Visions as radiant and rhapsodic as Kinnell's have difficulty confining themselves within the bounds of language. Though the poet seems at first to have sacrificed clarity in the search for sweep, rereadings of the poem disclose an intricately managed structure that unfolds in clarity as well as in intensity. I am not sure its conclusion is altogether worthy of what has led up to it, partly because Kinnell's hortatory style is better suited to rising incantation than to the dying fall, and I had a feeling at the end of having been thrown off while at full gallop. But it's an impressive piece of work by any standard.

The visions that arise in James Wright's *Collected Poems* (1971) are more paradisal than nightmarish. They have a way of rising out of their imagery on wings. The world for Wright is seen less as a solitary pilgrimage than as a garden of earthly delights. His poems are full of farm animals, scarecrows, owls, grass, and trees whose tops reach up to heaven, though their roots are fastened to the planet. He holds his being at the edge between earth and air. The barrier between the two is the force of gravity. The poet is seeking grace to overcome gravity's inhibitions.

> Now I am speaking with the voice
> of a scarecrow that stands up
> and suddenly turns into a bird.
> ("Listening to the Mourners")

*157*

A vision need not be forged out of irreconcilable opposites. Though there be anguish, to which Wright is no stranger, in the human condition, his anguish is envisioned merely as a part of the way things are, or even as a path to what is coming:

> Water is a luminous
> Mirror of swallows' nests. The stars
> Have gone down.
> What does my anguish
> Matter?
> ("Lighting Illegal Nets by Flashlight")

Wright's poems settle into symbols that lie sleeping in the grass of his Midwestern landscape—sights that may turn into insights, visibilities that may turn into visions if only they can be freed from their mortal limitations. He will have none of Kinnell's paradoxical nightmares, nor, say, of Sylvia Plath's murderous reconciliation of opposed forces. His is a simpler vision, one of heaviness and lightness, of rising and falling.

> An owl rises
> from the cutter bar
> of a hayrake.
> ("A Message Hidden in an Empty Wine Bottle
> That I Threw into a Gully of Maple Trees
> One Night at an Indecent Hour")

> We clattered the dung forks
> Beneath the dank joists
> Where, surely, somewhere,
> The nest curled over the blue
> Veins of somebody's
> Throat and wings.
> ("A Summer Memory in the Crowded City")

Wright unites the vision with the visionary so that what the poet sees rises naturally from what he is. The art is one of making the difficult look easy. He is not concerned with squeezing blood from stones or imposing the ravenous imperatives of his struggle for sanity on the processes of growing up and dying down. It is as much a part of his vision to aspire to rise as to fail and fall.

> I looked down
> And felt my wings waving aside the air,
> Furious to fly. For I could never bear
> Belly and breast and thigh against the ground.
> > ("The Angel")

> If I stepped out of my body I would break
> Into blossom.
> > ("A Blessing")

Death stands in a natural relation to life, without needing to be rammed into the same bed with it. Death is simply the last failure to rise above the animal condition, whether by force of accident or through ordinary mortality:

> I do not pity the dead. I pity the dying.
> > ("At the Executed Murderer's Grave")

> The girl flopped in the water like a pig
> And drowned dead drunk.
> > ("All the Beautiful are Blameless")

Wright does not seek to call attention to the strenuousness of his effort to comprehend, or to shout, "Look at me!" It is enough for him to steal glimpses of visions as they emerge, to catch them by surprise. This way he induces us to look at nature afresh, to find traces of our own features in the portraits of ordinary people. If at his weakest his manner is so ordinary as to be altogether unremarkable, at his strongest he can remind us of what we have always known but never noticed and reassure us that we have been there before. His visions do not need to transport us to a new country: they renew the old country for us. Wright's is, if you like, a pastoral vision. Still, mortality looms so large in it that smugness finds no entrance; and unlike most contemporary poetry, his leaves us room for love—as in his superb translation of Apollinaire's "The Pretty Redhead," where we find the lines:

All we want is to explore kindness the enormous country where everything is silent.

Weave a circle round him thrice.

# Poets of Exile and Isolation: Walcott, Koch, Simic, and Carruth

Since the invention of print the challenge to poets has been the widening gulf between the poet's sensibility and the receptivity of readers. Now and then in English, as with Pope, Wordsworth, Tennyson, Whitman, and Frost, the poet has succeeded in resonating, in his lifetime, with a large body of readers who then decide that *that* was poetry, and anything that comes after it cannot be. So the new poet who follows the old must recreate the language for himself every time be begins. He must even recreate himself as a speaker.

Derek Walcott, of Saint Lucia and Trinidad, probably the best-known English-language poet to emerge from the Caribbean, has been writing since he was eighteen in a mode that has changed surprisingly little in thirty-six years and in a language that takes its principal literary influence from the British Isles. His poetry sounds of the ocean, as you might expect from an islander, but as his rhythms wash out and wash in along the circling shores on which he imagines himself to stand, the reader feels circularly unattended, abandoned, unaccompanied, alone, as in the poems of Matthew Arnold. Seldom can there have been a comparable body of work that was so accomplished in terms of sound, so versatile in reaching out for information and allusion, so rich in music, and yet so often barren of ideas, so plangently lonely and lost and (here Walcott is unlike Arnold) so lacking in intimacy.

At first the reader of Walcott's *Collected Poems (1948–1984)*

*Washington Post Book World,* April 13, 1986.

feels a little like a listener in Conrad, seated on a teak deck at twilight to hear the endless unfolding of an ironic and imperial narrative. But it turns out to be a narrative without recognizable characters and limited in emotion, and the night wears on as the moon rises over silvery water and coasts across the sky and sets at last behind the trees, and all the while, interrupted now and then by the gasp of smoke from a dwindling cheroot, the voice goes on on and on. "Once," it seems to be saying with a sigh, "there was an island." In this vast book, notably in the four-thousand-line autobiographical poem, *Another Life* (1973), the monotony of Walcott's trade winds becomes nearly stifling and occasionally topples over into fustian; but in later volumes like *Sea Grapes* (1976) and *The Star-Apple Kingdom* (1979) the poet seems to have distanced himself from island life enough to bring perspective to the scene and more individuation to the voices he speaks in. The theme, however, remains:

> There were still shards of an ancient pastoral
> in those shires of the island where the cattle drank
> their pools of shadow from an older sky,
> surviving from when the landscape copied such subjects as
> "Herefords at Sunset in the Valley of the Wye."
>
> ("The Star-Apple Kingdom")

Isolation and exile will no doubt obsess Walcott as he continues varying his powerful theme. The oeuvre as a whole might suitably carry a title as Conradian as "Outcast of the Islands." In his own words,

> . . . I have only one theme:
> The bowsprit, the arrow, the longing, the lunging heart—
> the flight to a target whose aim we'll never know,
> vain search for one island that heals with its harbour. . . .
>
> ("The Schooner *Flight*")

∾

Kenneth Koch's poetry has, for me, succeeded best when it was funniest, as in his two long Byronic poems, *Ko, or A Season on Earth* (1960) and *The Duplications* (1977). His newest book, *On the Edge,* itself made up of two long poems, does not entertain. The first, "Impressions of Africa," will not tell you much about the continent except for its hotels; and when it ventures out of doors it sounds like a travel diary both in banality and off-handedness:

> The lion's muscles
> Are amazing. The air
> Is filled with lions' grace.
> Viewed without any
> Human component around,
> The lion is sensational
> Simply of and in himself.

Some lion. Some sensation. Nowadays Koch is writing poems in which nearly every appearance of Poetry is to be avoided. The second poem, "On the Edge," will be read, I fear, only by people whose curiosity about Koch's autobiography comes from being mentioned in it; but that will make quite a crowd. His world is the Rialto of art openings, European travel, international *affaires de coeur*. This poem depends almost entirely on allusions of the sort that, in high school, seemed calculated to exclude outsiders, to make the nonbelonger feel stupid, to make the reader ransack for a footnote:

> Harry walks with me through the show of roses.
> We talk about Maxine. Elizabeth
> Is dancy at my side, as she supposes
> I like her. I am somewhat out of breath.
> With Jean I walk along and the place closes.
> We dance beside the Marne. I love my desk.
> As a drowning man to a spar I hold on to my desk. (F. Kafka)

As a memoir of *temps perdus*, "On the Edge" cannot hold a candle to scores of L. E. Sissman's worldly elegies, nor can Koch's attempts to peek around the edges of reality match the work of his admiring friend John Ashbery, who deems Koch, according to the jacket, "one of our greatest poets." If only Koch, self-serious, elegant, solipsistic, *degagé*, had continued to exercise his gift for satire, for clowning, for merriment. When he does so he is one of the most amusing poets we have.

~

Is a poet better off isolated or exiled? Koch sometimes seems isolated among the tricks of the "New York School" of poets. Charles Simic, by contrast, stands in a different part of the forest, one of the foremost doyens of the "new surrealists," the school of the present tense, poets who owe as much to César Vallejo as to William Carlos Williams, combining American simplicity with shreds of European surrealism. Simic, born in Yugoslavia in 1938, embodies the powers of the alone-in-the-world poets, nearly all male, who write poems hardly populated, hardly impassioned, mad for clarity, withdrawn, often slightly paranoid in their exclusion of characters and events. Here are some examples from *Selected Poems, 1963–1983:*

> Time slopes. We are falling head over heels
> At the speed of night. That milk tooth
> You left under the pillow, it's grinning.
> > ("What the White Had to Say")

> A cup of herb tea with a bride's eyelash
> Floating in it.
> > ("Rosalia")

> A plain black cotton dress
> On a wire hanger
> In a closet otherwise empty,
> Its door ajar to the light.
> > ("Piety")

These samples of Simic's work hint at his vision of poetry: a seeing eye that somehow penetrates surfaces:

> There are windows
> And blackboards,
> One can only see through
> With eyes closed.
> > ("School for Dark Thoughts")

Simic's poetry does not do very much for or with the ear or with the senses beyond vision; nor does it reach out with much compassion, nor does it connect events into narrative. Most of the contemporary poets who are doing such things are, as it turns out, women. Many male poets nowadays seem to be writing themselves into a corner, into willed isolation, into a world beyond the vanishing point, into "another republic," to use words that Charles Simic and Mark Strand once used to entitle an anthology.

Hayden Carruth, born in 1921, comes out of an earlier generation, those old enough to have served and suffered in World War II. He has just published a volume of *Selected Poetry,* edited and introduced by Galway Kinnell. Something in the sensibility of his war-slashed generation preserved in male poetry some of the compassionate and familial attitudes of women, the sort of thing that our best women poets—May Swenson, Margaret Atwood, Carolyn Kizer, Mary Oliver, Ellen Bryant Voigt, Louise Glück, Tess Gallagher, Gjertrud Schnackenberg—weave into their poetry as a matter of course: mercy, pity, peace, and love. I cannot imagine any of the previous poets discussed here writing such a line as "How gravely and sweetly the poor touch in the dark" ("If It Were Not For You"). That is pure Carruth. Or this:

> And when it was given to me, a rude gift to hurt me,
> I was not hurt, but thankful and pleased to possess
>     something.
> I worked with my shaping hands, molding and caressing,
> To make a beautiful stone, and it has grown ever
> More in grace and love, my image, my stone, my girl
> Who makes me and shapes me as I turn her form
> In my hands; I am the partner of the stone.
>                     (from "The Bloomingdale Papers")

Carruth's work, as Kinnell points out in an eloquent and heartfelt foreword, touches the reader by touching other people, characters, personae, sometimes in eclogues like Frost's, sometimes in poems about jazz, about work, about, in fact, the preoccupations of the poor, the excluded, the shut-out and shut-in. By reaching out to others, though the poet remain in exile, he heals his isolation. A poem like "Regarding Chainsaws" invites comparison with the Frost canon; poems like "The Bloomingdale Papers" give Carruth's voice a pathos as affecting as John Berryman's, though less affected. His love poems and his country poems convey a fleshly delight that any reader, professional or amateur, can respond to:

> Like a broken telephone a cricket rings
> without assertion in dead asters and
> goldenrod; asters gone cloudy with seed,
> goldenrod burnt and blackened.
>
> ("Once More")

Carruth's poems have the ring of clarity because they have the generous ring of himself. I don't know much about Carruth's life except what his poems reveal, which is quite a lot; but his virtue, whether you regard it as a quality of character or of talent, is not to regard himself—how unlike so many other poets!—as a special case. He does not isolate himself in a single special angle of vision, nor does he single out one part of the sensibility. It tries to enlist the whole man, the whole of his existence, and it brings into play all his senses, all his intelligence, his madness, and his sorrow. What more can a poet give? How many poets give so much?

# The Sanity of *Human Wishes:*
# Robert Hass

On the poetry circuit, in the college-town bars, faculty cafeterias and California coffee shops, they have been waiting a decade for this book. Robert Hass, more than any other poet now in his forties, performs what other American poets of his generation have been yearning to emulate. In this respect, as in his capacity to convey pleasure in poetry, he fills the place of the late Elizabeth Bishop. Stanley Kunitz years ago wrote: "Reading a poem by Robert Hass is like stepping into the ocean when the temperature of the water is not much different from that of the air. You scarcely know, until you feel the undertow tug at you, that you have entered into another element."[1]

Hass's first volume, *Field Guide,* more than any other poetic debut of the 1970s, took up new postures: it seemed so fulfilled in its assurance, its care, its originality of authorship, its gentleness, its wit, its firmness of indignation. Those poems catalogued the phenomena of the California natural order, they spoke of family ties, of political injustice, of the rewards and challenges of literature. Hass's second volume, *Praise* (1979), had in it at least one masterpiece ("Heroic Simile") and one other poem, "Meditation at Lagunitas," which served a

---

Part in *The Atlantic Monthly,* June, 1979, under the title "The Great Predicament of Poetry," and part in the *Boston Globe,* September 24, 1989.
[1]From the Introduction to Robert Hass, *Field Guide* (New Haven: Yale University Press, 1973).

generation as an aesthetic model. "All the new thinking is about loss," he remarked disarmingly:

> In this it resembles all the old thinking.
> The idea, for example, that each particular erases
> the luminous clarity of a general idea.

*Praise* lit up the transition from the social entanglements of the poetry of the 1970s to the self-regard of the 1980s. Poem after poem set limits for itself as stern as gravity: white on white, block on block of stone, frames around pictures. The very motionlessness of the visual arts played a part in Hass's aesthetic ("It's an advantage of paintings"), as did the minutiae of nature:

> . . . What I want happens
> not when the deer freezes in the shade
> and looks at you and you hold very still
> and meet her gaze but in the moment after
> when she flicks her ears & starts to feed again.
>
> ("Santa Lucia")

*Praise* also fell, now and then, into the trap of formulaic self-description that American poets are now trying to write their way out of: Hass's poetic intelligence was so acute that he kept, like Hamlet, cerebrating himself into the static condition that turned out to be all that his verbs would allow him. Regardless of his protestations to the contrary, his poems too seldom broke out of the straight subject-predicate construction and kept getting stuck in the is-ness of their situations. It is not surprising that he concentrates upon pictures, paintings, sculptures, motionless images, even in his very finest poems, such as "Heroic Simile," one of the most remarkable single poems of recent years.

Hass also brought together a book of luminous criticism, *Twentieth-Century Pleasures* (1984), that won the National Book Critics Circle Award and explicated his own formal and aesthetic intentions. He has translated, with Robert Pinsky, many of the poems of the Nobel Laureate Czeslaw Milosz, and he was awarded a MacArthur Fellowship.

Now, with *Human Wishes*, the wait is over. Hass's work has climbed to a place of the first importance in American poetry. This book shows the poet learning about aspiration from his children, Leif, Kristin, and Luke; exploring the consequences of desire with his wife and other women; describing with affectionate sadness the decline of a marriage and its expectations. His work is suffused with love, tinted with the balminess of the northern California climate, cradled in a balance of emotion that owes much to Buddhist acceptance, swept by a passion for language that treats words, form, ideas, with the shaping affection of handwork.

Human wishes are expressed in sex, family, responses to phenomena in nature, and by means of long linked phrases that take us to the heart of sensuous occurrences that resonate simultaneously in the real world, in imagination, in the past:

> because desires do not split themselves up, there is one desire
> touching the many things, and it is continuous.
>
> ("Natural Theology")

Hass's poetry acts

> as if language were a kind of moral cloud chamber through
> which the world passed and from which it emerged charged
> with desire.
>
> ("Human Wishes")

His poems participate in situations in which men and women, often seated around a kitchen table and drinking coffee (*coffee* is one of Hass's magic words), observe children discovering their relation to the world, and thereby teaching their parents what the world is like.

> You gather sadness
> from a childhood to make a gift of it.
>
> ("Berkeley Eclogue")

So much for subject matter. How does the singular quality of Hass's poetry show?

> You notice rhythms
> washing over you, opening and closing,
> they are the world, inside you, and you work.
>
> ("Santa Lucia II")

The first section of this book takes the form of adages or sentences, the second part, prose poems. Most contemporary prose poems lack shape, like water carried in a sieve, but Hass's are among the few that hold the water of their author's style. The concluding two sections of *Human Wishes* are written in verse: part 3 dwells on past happiness; part 4, on present resignation.

Most typical of Hass's poems are Vermeer-like pictures of the sweet unfolding melancholy of domestic life, in which the figures look out at the reader, their leisured postures emanating a Zen-like patience about the passage of time, as in a prose poem called "Museum":

> But this young couple is reading the Sunday paper in the sun, the baby is sleeping, the green has begun to emerge from the rind of the canteloupe, and everything seems possible.

*Human Wishes* takes Hass's poetry to a level of tenderness that few of his contemporaries have reached, mainly because it eschews complaint. It accepts, it embraces, it inhales love and loss, the smell of coffee, the sweetness of sex, beauty, and terror alike, the depths of sorrow and loss, and the exaltation of the heights, as little poetry has done since the death of James Wright.

> Things bloom up there. They are
> for the season alive in those bright vanishings
> of air we ran through.
>
> ("On Squaw Peak")

I cannot think of any other living poet who could have written those lines, balanced as they are between the aesthetics of

East and West. Hass brings us a unique yet wholly recognizable vision of the world, a vision that admits tragedy, morality, and outrage into its sensuous yet mild-mannered way of speaking, and rhythms that stamp a hallmark on his work. It would be no surprise if he turned out to be one of our major poets, for he has all the requisites: intelligence, depth, musicality, sweep, intimacy, humor, observation, learning, and, above all, compassion.

# Lucia Maria Perillo: *Dangerous Life*

Sometimes, while reading a large quantity of poetry, a single poem—if it be in the work of one poet or in an anthology, or in this case in a pile of manuscripts to be judged in a competition—suddenly rises up from its fellows and takes command. In my reading for the 1989 Morse Prize such a poem appeared near the beginning of my work: it was "Jury Selection," a poem about a notorious case of multiple rape that occurred in New Bedford, Massachusetts, several years ago at a bar called "Big Dan's."

> She says she only went in for a minute
> to tug on the silver nozzles of the cigarette machine, but
> the thin curtains that line her bedroom windows
> are clearly visible from the street. The whole town knows.
> Even some of these young men
> carry the blue nickels of her thumbprints on the backs of
> their thighs from this time,
> but also the times before . . .
>
> We all do violence.

There are better poems, no doubt, in this collection than "Jury Selection," but this one first alerted me to its author's remarkable qualities: a command of imagery (those blue nickels), a true ear for the demotic, a power to rise above the merely autobiographical. *Dangerous Life* impresses me, after many readings, because of its fierce consistency, for the way it will not

---

Introduction to *Dangerous Life* by Lucia Maria Perillo (Boston: Northeastern University Press, 1989), winner of the 1989 Morse Poetry Prize.

turn its back on fear, a woman's fear of the violence in her destiny. A thousand tracts excoriating society's addiction to violence cannot equal the chilling effect of these poems: they leave a taste of metal in the mouth. Try "Fire Bomber" or "Photojournalism" or "Diptych: The Milk Carton Children" or "Field Guide to the Dead & Dying Flowers of Eastern North America" or "The News (A Manifesto)" or "Deflowering: Three Rites."

I know nothing of Lucia Maria Perillo except her poems (though I expect readers of poetry will be hearing more of her). They testify to an Italo-American upbringing in the Bronx but take us on journeys across our continent in search of freedom from the fear that will not vanish:

> But I kept the merit badge marked *Dangerous Life,*
> for which, if you remember, the girls were taken to the
> woods and taught the mechanics of fire,
>
> around which they had to dance with pointed sticks . . .
> ("Dangerous Life")

Such fear will not vanish in a present where people play deadly games at parties ("Two Parties") or at work ("First Job") or in the intimacies of female life ("Bags") or in the menace of industrialization ("Cesium: for Goiania, Brazil, September 30, 1987"), or in the ways we pursue love ("Logotherapy: After Betrayal," or "Gauntlet").

"Sometimes," Perillo writes, "I feel history slipping from my body / like a guilty bone," but she insists on keeping track of it, blocking its escape. Her instincts are remarkable for the way they seek out the detail that tells, especially the incident that tells: a young girl swimming in a polluted river; a teenage girl set free, then chastened, by driving too fast; the firebombing (by another teenager) of a gloomy old church and its replacement by a bland new one,

> Every month they'd bring around a troop of well-scrubbed
>     teenagers
> in shimmering yellow suits and dresses, to play guitars and
>     sing *Kum-bay-ya;*
> ("Firebomber")

she tells of a disturbing relationship with a brother—and she knows the fear of danger for what it is, has the honesty to tell us how it "still gives me a small rush of joy." And there is pride too, justified pride in

> . . . enduring, keeping what few secrets lie inside of you inside
>     of you: heroic myths, ugly rumors—
> about God and about some ancient rites of spring.
>                     ("Field Guide to the Dead and Dying Flowers
>                             of Eastern North America")

As you may gather, this book concentrates its attention on the rites of passage that take us out of adolescence into whatever we call its aftermath. Maturity? Adulthood? It happens. We survive. But ultimately the pride evinced in this fascinating and altogether readable volume has less to do with the pride of surviving adolescence than the pride of the poet. Homer has Alcinoüs, the king of the Phaeacians, praise Odysseus:

> You speak with art, but your intent is honest.
> The Argive troubles, and your own troubles,
> you told as a poet would, a man who knows the world.

Lucia Maria Perillo, like any good poet, knows the world, and she speaks with art, reciting the truths and rhythms that have reinforced her pride:

> Some nights I take my lanyards from their shoebox,
>                             practice baying
> those old campsongs to the moon. And remember how they
>                             told us
> that a smart girl could find her way out of anywhere, alive.

# IV

# Self-Appraisal

# Poems Happen

The worst danger in making an example of yourself is making a fool of yourself, but I have found, after seventeen years as an editor of books, that almost no generalizations are valid about the ways writers get their work done. Early in the morning, late at night; regularly scheduled hours, irregular bursts of work; pen, pencil, typewriter; slow composition incorporating revisions sentence by sentence; fast composition requiring draft after draft; or, most enviable of all, Bertrand Russell's method, which is rapid composition with no need to revise a word. All these methods are possible, and all are successfully employed by one writer or another.

The only reliable information I can pass on, therefore, is about myself. I was an editor of books for years before I became a writer, but I have always adored the craft of writing in both capacities. Though I loved editing, I always felt in my heart that writing was the most rewarding thing in the world to do. I strove, I strained, I failed. Nothing I wrote was ever finished. I began novels, essays; I kept journals but abandoned them after a few weeks. I invented exercises to make myself go on, but to no effect. All through those years I was happily advising other writers—sometimes helpfully—and encouraging other people's work. I could do nothing for mine.

What can be more difficult to describe than the process of creation? Good writing is not easy. It requires all the pain and labor of heaving coal below decks in a hurricane, as Joseph Conrad, who had done both, contended. However, once the way is found, the beginning of writing contains the true sim-

---

*The Writer,* August, 1967, under the title "Time and the Poet."

plicity of great mysteries. "If a man," Coleridge once wrote, "could pass through Paradise as in a dream, and have a flower presented to him as a pledge that his soul had really been there, and if he found that flower in his hand when he awoke—Ay! and what then?"

What then, indeed? In 1957, when I was twenty-nine and had still written nothing, I was sitting on a screened-in porch above the treetops on an August Sunday afternoon, reading in manuscript, preparatory to their publication, *The Selected Poems of Stanley Kunitz*. The powerful resonance of Kunitz's work must have released something, for I suddenly found that my first poem was happening to me. "Happening" is the only word for it. I got it on paper, revised it twenty times over the next months, and it was duly published in *The Atlantic*, and ultimately in my first book.

### The Winner

I hear a child inside,
Crying to be let out.
"No," shouts the swaggering self,
"Mind shall destroy all doubt.
Doubt shall not interfere.
Stifle that treacherous word.
I have high deeds to do,
Twirling my deathly sword."

Mind's on his mettle now,
Deft at his surgical art,
Stunning my pain with pain,
Drowning the infant heart.

I found myself, at age twenty-nine, helplessly involved with making myself ready to write poems when they should occur; and, equally, as a publisher, committed to one of the most demanding and time-consuming of occupations. Editing absorbed me, and I now know it always will. I have for many years put in a long editorial work day, which begins well before nine and goes on well beyond five. When I started writing poems, I thought all that would change, but it has not. Now that I look back on it, I'm still a bit surprised at how little the externals of my life have altered. There was no planning to it, for I had no choice.

Poems happen. A poet's first task is to be ready when they happen. Not over-ready, not a hair-trigger tension to fire at every murmur in the darkness; but ready for the real poems, when the accidental events of life and imagination cast them up for the intelligence to look at. A poet must always be ready for these moments, and he pays a high price in frustration and blighted composition if he is not. Sleeping and waking, working or idling, he must be alert to the first suggestion, the first surge of a new poem, and he must get it—or some shorthand version of it—down on paper soon, before it recedes into the darkness whence it came. If he can do this, the rest has a chance to follow. But this readiness is not a matter of time spent, of hard work, of blood, sweat, and tears, or of efficiency. It is, simply, a state of consciousness.

My own favorite time for writing—or for revision, to be more exact—is weekend mornings when the house is quiet and the children are outdoors. I am lucky enough to have a workroom of my own, yet noise would not interrupt me at times like these. (The telephone would, and the telephone at these times is not answered unless my wife answers it.) I open my notebook and find, sometimes to my surprise, poems and notes for poems that may have been accumulating for days or weeks. I start to work on the one that catches my fancy. I shape it—rewriting, copying, changing words, rhythms, punctuation, then recopying—until I am tired and can do no more without injuring the poem by over-attention. Then I turn to the next poem and do the same. A few fortunate poems have been finished after one or two turns at this treatment; others have remained at this stage for years before finally emerging; some never will.

The time to write? The time to write is infinite. You can never have enough; yet it is quite possible to have too much. For me writing time is measured on a different scale, a different continuum from the rest of my world. Five minutes of pure attention to an emerging poem is longer than a week of clocks and hours. I am lucky to be given my openings, and I shamelessly exploit them. To glance at the flower in my hand is proof enough that I passed through Paradise.

# Praying Wrong: An Interview

[The following interview concentrated on the theme of prayer in my selected poems, *Praying Wrong*. My Author's Note in that book begins: "Nearly all poems utter a prayer, whether explicit or not, a plea for some sort of consequence, even if it's no more than a call for order or a complaint to the management."]

*What is the function of prayer, in your view?*

I've always been fascinated by Spinoza's notion that the only proper function of prayer is songs of praise. If God is infinite, how can you ask him finite questions? How can you ask him to grant a wish—a home run, a free throw? In fact it's inappropriate and insulting, Spinoza seems to say, to ask God to grant anything. So perhaps we simply deceive ourselves by asking for things. Lord knows we seldom get them, or not what we want. There is an old saw that no good deed goes unpunished.

*Do you think that prayers have positive psychological effects on a person?*

Of course: especially if they are sung. It seems to me you should just pray away. At least prayer enables you to find out, as I say in one of my poems, what it is you *think* you want. I don't know how efficacious it is beyond that. After all, praying is one of the first things we ever seem to do in this world: the moment we come out of the womb we open our mouths and

A radio interview with Rachel Berghash recorded by WBAI-FM, New York, for broadcast on June 30, 1985.

pray for something: we wawl and cry, as Lear says. It may be a protest, saying, GOD STOP THIS COLD or it may signify GOD I WANT MILK. We cannot remember what that first cry meant, but our first act on this earth is not silent.

*Do you find that prayers are being answered not in the way we ask them but in any other way?*

All the time. That's very treacherous. The typical fairy tale is one in which the person who is given three wishes asks for the wrong thing: the man who had a dumb wife and wishes she could speak and lives to regret it. The princes who come to woo Portia in *The Merchant of Venice* all ask for the wrong thing. Nobody ever asks the right question. If you ask for the wrong casket you might get the right girl, as, in Shakespeare, he who chooses the leaden casket wins Portia. But to do that is almost perverse. It is like asking for what you *don't* want.

*I think that prayer works. It is one of the reasons why I am fascinated by the excellent title of your book,* Praying Wrong, *and your poems about prayer. The topic is very interesting because you have to be very careful about what you pray for, because you are going to get it.*

That's right: you may. But if you get what you don't want you can either blame fate, or you can blame yourself for having prayed wrong. That's why we have to be pretty careful about what words we use; and that's why we might even call the art of poetry the art of praying wrong.

*In your poem "Wordless Winter" you don't want to be forgiven for whatever wrong you think you may have done. I understand that, but most people think it is odd not to want to be forgiven.*

If you've lost something or somebody whom you loved very dearly, it may turn out to be impossible for you to admit to yourself that there wasn't one more thing you could have done to prevent it. Do you dare forgive yourself for it? What has happened is so awful, so terrible, that it lies beyond forgiveness, and you have no right to forgive yourself. You can eventually come to peace with yourself, but what you've lost is irrecoverably lost. There is a wonderful poem by Robert Hass, "Meditation at Lagunitas," which begins: "All the new thinking is about loss. In this // it resembles all the old thinking." It's what we express in the primal birth cry: the first thing we know on earth is loss, the loss of security in the womb. Somehow we have partly persuaded ourselves that we can "have it all," if we only believe the Michelob ad. We claim that we can make anything we want of ourselves. We assert that there is no barrier to our creativity or our originality. How do we reconcile that heresy with the fact that we are born to change, we are born to loss, we are born to die? Very pompous, no?

*When Yeats said that "those who love are sad," I think he was thinking of loss; because when you love, you are always connected with the idea that you might lose the person.*

What he took first is

> . . . the supreme theme of Art and Song:
> Bodily decrepitude is wisdom; young
> We loved each other and were ignorant.

*In your poem "The Vanishing Point" you say,*

> Each moment wishes us to move farther on
> into a sequence we can follow at most to vanishing point.

*What are the consequences of only seeing to vanishing point?*

I'm afraid it is as far as we *can* see; it's as far as the curve of the earth will let us see. It is part of the nature of being only human. The consequences of that are that some things cannot be seen at all without possessing second sight. When I open a dictionary I haven't seen before, I look up the word *vision.* The more the definition has to do with optics and the less it has to do with mysticism, the less desirable I find the dictionary. The very technological dictionaries will mostly deal with optics, and when they talk about visionaries they'll suggest that visions are a delusion, something that cannot be trusted, an aberration. I prefer visions, visions like:

> A damsel with a dulcimer
> In a vision once I saw:
> It was an Abyssinian maid,
> And on her dulcimer she played,
> Singing of Mount Abora.

If we could see beyond vanishing point, we could see not only beyond the horizon but into the future, into the past, into all those places that in fact are forbidden to us as we live here, trapped in three dimensions. Poetry has a lot to do with seeing around corners.

*You write in "Paradise as a Garden":*

> Whatever persists within, forever fresh,
> is the indelible border of imagination.

*And in "The Woodcock" you write:*

> Regardless of the gifts we've left behind
> and all the boundaries we cannot cross,
> some power lets us press beyond our powers . . .

*What is that power that sometimes strengthens us, so that we have the power to see beyond the vanishing point?*

The metaphor here is not one of seeing. "The Woodcock" concludes with a passage about how, when we took to the woods, we no longer needed to see very far; trees were in the way. I meant to speak in evolutionary terms. We gave up our fins, which became feathers. When birds became able to fly, they did not need weapons to defend themselves, or hard outward coverings, because they were now able simply to fly away from danger. The woodcock cannot, in fact, see very well by day, and thus it comes out at the edge of dark for its mating flight. The male goes up in spirals singing all kinds of extraordinary things, and the female (or so I believe) sits on the ground like Molly Bloom saying, as it were, "yes yes yes." The male woodcock makes me a metaphor of singing, praying, poetry, or whatever we like to call such activities of exaltation; sex, among other things, enables us to "press beyond our powers," for the sake of winning the muse, who crouches in the shrubbery literally egging us on. The flight isn't an act of understanding in the visionary sense, but in the cantatory sense, in the sense of singing. Why is it that poetry seems to be such an impractical art, so easily and happily neglected? (I have reasons for feeling rather glad about that, by the way.) Why is it that we can cast our little spells and sing our little songs, knowing in fact that these incantations ("Weave a circle round him thrice . . .") enable us to see farther, by some strange means. "Seeing" is the word I keep falling into when I do not mean *sight* but *vision*. Yet there is something about sound that is inseparable from vision, at least in my kind of poetry. There is something incantatory, something rhythmic, something to do with song, that makes vision of this kind possible.

*Does it evoke the sight?*

Second sight. Like prayer wheels in Tibet. When people sing they want to evoke a higher frame of being, even if the burden of the song is only, "Hey I want you," or "Don't you act so mean to me Mama." Singing tries to change reality, to lay a charm on it. It yearns to enable us to receive what we desire.

*Poetry in its origin was oral.*

Of course, in every civilization. But when it becomes a written art—to the extent it does—poetry helps us *press beyond our powers*. It gets us somehow beyond our five senses.

*Did I hear you say that you are happy that poetry is for the few?*

Not for the few. I said I am a little happy that poetry is *neglected*. That which is neglected doesn't get interfered with. There's no money in it. People will leave us alone, to go on doing what we're doing, so that, if we are any good, the poems won't escape, won't get away, and sometime, later on, people will remember what we said, what we wrote. Robert Frost used to say that he hoped he could write a few poems that would stick like burs under a saddle. When Milton talks about fame—"That last infirmity of noble mind"—he addresses a whole poem to Lycidas, a man he protests he loves; but in fact all he does is talk about himself, about how deeply he hopes someone will remember what he said. Well, we do remember what he said because he cared so much about being remembered, and his desire partakes so deeply of the human voice; but we also notice the poem's moral insincerity.

*What you are leading to is that name and fame corrupt. They can corrupt even the poets.*

Yes. Corruption is a function of society, not of poetry. Poets, God knows, are just as capable of being corrupted as anyone else. What poets are good at is singing, not virtue.

*I thought it was in the poet not to be corrupted.*

Let us hope that the *art* remains incorrupted. But I don't think that anyone who knows poets well would claim that many of them are incorruptible. Far from it.

*You write about change. What are your feelings when you write, "Change is all?" Do you resist it, or participate in it?*

I wonder to what extent we should want to hurry change along. People now are always trying to speed the pace of social change, if they are reformers, or progressives, or technologists, or revolutionaries. They retain enough optimism to believe that they can improve the universe through their own unaided efforts. Yet it is the poet who insists, "The paths of glory lead but to the grave." I certainly see no point in protesting the future. On the other hand I see no point in hurrying along with it simply because it's on the move. If you think of life as a river and yourself in a boat paddling downstream, the harder you paddle the sooner you get to the end. But should we want to be finished so quickly? I once edited a book, *Cosmic Dawn,* by the astronomer Eric Chaisson, who repeatedly made the point that there is only one constant to be encountered in the fifteen billion years of the universe: that change occurs. Regardless of how badly we want to believe in the static, the eternal, in fact we begin in loss and continue in change. Loss is all. Change is all.

*Do you think we can take the direction of the change? It could be either in the direction of healing or in the direction of decay?*

I am not sure whether we have much choice in the matter. Not as individuals. We might hope that people who have visionary capability, as poets are supposed to, might be able to know whether to strike out across the current, or upstream against it, or downstream with it. But I don't have much confidence in the historical or ethical, or even biological, prescience of poets.

*Do you think that one could be motivated by love to take a certain direction?*

If you love someone, you want to protect that person—those people, those children. I certainly imagine *that* as being a "good" motivation. But there can be terrible corruptions of family love, like everything else. I think that too much love of the unborn child, taken to its extreme, can manifest itself in hatred of the living. If for example society is trying to salvage two- or three-month fetuses, which are unviable, and condemn living adults to dedicate forty or fifty or sixty years of their lives to taking care of creatures who are unfit to take care of themselves. . . . That's a quite specific and rather agonizing example of what I mean by the corruption of love.

*In your poem "Having Saints" there is the idea of prayer. I am wondering whether you think that certain saints are good at certain things, therefore we can pray to them about these things, their specialties. For instance, St. Teresa of Avila had to work very hard to be a saint; while St. John of the Cross was a natural. Should we direct our prayers that way?*

I think of minor saints like St. Blaise, known in Italy as San Biagio, who is the patron saint of sore throats. If you get strep, pray to San Biagio. Or St. Botolph, the patron saint of Boston, in Lincolnshire, who seems to have been in charge of successful river crossings at a certain ford. And St. Christopher, the patron saint of travelers. In the heyday of medieval sanctity, there was a saint for everything, and everything had its saint. I'm amused by what the legends of saints tell us about our desires. It's nice to make up saints according to need. Who would be chosen as the patron saint of computer programmers? Of floppy-disk makers? Of compatibility? Which saint is friendly to users?

*Saints would be a kind of legitimating authority in straightening out scrambled programs?*

Good idea. I don't know much about the processes of beatification, but, as I recall, a saint's sponsors have to prove that the candidate for sainthood has performed miracles, that special holiness attached to certain aspects of his or her life; and so on. . . . Finally Authority pronounces this person to be a saint and that person not. The one who got her breasts torn off by pincers is often enthusiastically depicted in Rome—I can't remember her name. Then there's St. Agatha, rather splendid. She was disrobed by barbarians, but her body immediately grew a great head-to-foot beard so that she wouldn't be seen naked. Could she be the saint of barbers?

*In "The Pleaders" the pleaders don't know how to ask or pray. Is it that they just don't know how, or are God and they on different wavelengths? And who are "the pleaders" anyhow?*

Those in my poem are the people in the street. People whom those in government and a position of power decide things for. The pleaders are people who get housing developments built for them without ever being consulted. The people whose demographic characteristics are defined by experts who then decide how to alter them. The pleaders are people who know how to pray, but not how to pray to *these* people, the people who have decided to lead them (or follow them, depending on how you regard leadership). If the pleaders knew how to pray to the leaders, they would tell the leaders what they want: but they don't know how to formulate those prayers. So the leaders give them what *they* think they want, which seldom if ever turns out to be what the people in fact wanted. Look at the most secular of situations today. The experts who want to build the Westway in New York have their reasons for wanting to build it, and they further their aims by trying to prove that the Westway will be good for everybody. But you know perfectly well who it's going to be best for: the people who are planning it.

> We are the eyes your eyes have never met.
> We are the voice you will not wait to hear.
> We are the part of you you have forgotten,
> Or trampled out, or lost and wept to lose.
> *We are your children, whom you treat like horses;*
> *We are among you; we are going to stay.*

During the radical years of the late sixties and early seventies, a certified radical said to me, "What do you mean, children are like horses?" But I saw him treat his children very much like horses, and nowadays the burden we put on the children of the poor is one of the scandals of American history. We wouldn't do that to a horse, not any more. You put burdens on them whether the burdens are literal or metaphorical.

*Beyond their capacity.*

Maybe beyond their capacity, maybe not. But you certainly teach them to obey a bridle, and carry saddles, and to pull weights. And those weights are not chosen by the horse. "We are your children, whom you treat like horses."

*Is anyone exempt? Is anyone in a privileged position?*

Nobody is. No. Even the poor millionaire has to worry about taxes, or about all the people who ask him for favors. What a shame. Does nobody love him for himself? "Only God, my dear, / Could love you for yourself alone / And not your yellow hair," as Yeats said.

*Could you talk about the line, "only in my flesh / shall I see God," in your poem "Two Midrashim"?*

I have trouble with the more austere ruminations of St. Paul—with putting the flesh aside. To me the Old Testament—from which those words come—is more sane in this regard.

*St. Teresa said that the body is the temple of the soul, so it is in Christianity as well.*

Of course it is. St. Francis speaks of it, most of the saints speak of it. When we talk about "visions" I can't abstract to one sense only, but I include all the senses, all the body. "Only in my flesh shall I see God"—it's a great moment in the Book of Job: "For I know that my redeemer liveth, and that he shall stand at the latter day upon the earth: and though after my skin worms destroy this body, yet in my flesh shall I see God" (19:25–26). Even though the body is gone you still "see God" in the flesh. "Beauty is momentary in the mind / The fitful tracing of a portal; / But in the flesh it is immortal." You could take that as a literal raising of the body after death, but I don't have to go that far.

*When I read the section "Willing Her to Live" from your poem "Wordless Winter," I think of the end of things—eschatology. Do you think it is a good idea to imagine the end of things, such as the end of life, the end of a marriage or of a job, so that when it comes you are prepared?*

I don't know whether it is a good idea to imagine the last things, but it may be more dangerous not to. To have these things come at you with a sense of complete surprise has some beauty to it, in the sense that Walt Whitman writes about the animals: "They do not sweat and whine about their condition." An animal seems not to anticipate the coming of death, and therefore it arrives as yet another surprise in a surprising life. Still, I think I would rather prepare for death. I've seen people organize their lives in such a way as to be ready. It's a beautiful sight. Lets say that—perhaps just for aesthetic reasons—it's not a bad idea to keep an eye on last things. I think we want our lives to have some shape to them—at least that's why I write poetry. I'd like to see if there is any shape in my life; and if there is a shape, can I recognize it? If there is a way in which vision, the sort of vision we have talked about, can help shape that life, I'd like to try. That's why there's an element of consecration in poetry, and in living, and in the relation between the two. My own vocabulary for this tends to take religious forms. I am not really sure whether I have "religious beliefs" or not. But the words of consecration are very beautiful, and they may possibly be efficacious, provided that we pray correctly!

*I'd like to go back to your poem "The Vanishing Point," where you say: "This present moment, exquisitely poised, / had not yet given in to the scramble of time." Could you talk about that?*

I think we all can remember times, moments in our life, whether they have been deeply significant moments or completely insignificant, in which time seemed to change its pace radically. I'm sure most of us, just before falling or having an accident or a car crash or watching a loved one about to come to harm, felt that time stopped, almost stopped, for a long time, and then gathered up and went forward again. This may have a relatively simple physical explanation, like the summoning of adrenaline, which alters the body's measurement of time. But what happens in those instances when there is no threat, when there is no danger? Does such a pause afford a glimpse around the corner, beyond the finite, some other kind of vision? Can we see objects beyond seeing, places we can experience without experiencing? "The Vanishing Point" deals with a particular moment on a completely uneventful morning, when something happened in the weather and struck my consciousness with the realization that time had stopped. That time I was able to wait and watch until it began again. It's the mystery, the endless mystery. In the middle of my poem "Questions of Swimming, 1935," I quote from Conrad's *Lord Jim:* "To the destructive element submit yourself, / and with the exertions of your hands and feet / make the deep, deep sea keep you up." In the midst of life we are in death, in the midst of destruction we are in life. That is the message of Primo Levi. My poems in "Walking the Boundaries" sketch the borderland between what's known and what's unknown. The boundary is only a line or a membrane, and occasionally permeable. It's those moments of seeing *just beyond* that make us rejoice when perhaps we have reasons to despair, and also make us despair when we have reasons to rejoice, because we learn from those moments that not everything is capable of solution. " 'No, not yet,' " as the world says at the end of *A Passage to India.* "And the sky said, 'No, not there.' "

# Self-Portrait:
## Sources, Impacts, Decisions

I was born in Lenox Hill Hospital in New York on June 27, 1928, unremarkably as far as I know, and came home on Independence Day to my parents' rented apartment in Brooklyn Heights. My father, Edward Davison, three weeks short of thirty, was a tousle-haired English poet, about six feet tall, possessed of more than enough charm to hold a crowd. Already the author of three published books of poetry and a volume of critical essays, he edited a weekly contributors' page in the new *Saturday Review of Literature* and had developed sufficient reputation as a speaker to excite demand on the women's club lecture circuit.

My mother, Natalie Weiner Davison, not yet twenty-nine, was buxom, auburn-haired, convivial, glowingly beautiful. Her childhood, unlike my father's, had been privileged, sheltered in an affluent and assimilated Jewish home with a younger sister on the upper West Side of Manhattan. My grandfather, Joseph Solomon Weiner, had immigrated to New York at seventeen, in 1887, from his birthplace in Trenčín, in what is now Czechoslovakia, leaving home like thousands of others to avoid Franz Josef's military conscription. He followed his elder brothers to New York and before long found prosperity as their partner in Weiner Brothers of Spring Street, Cotton Goods. This in time made him eligible to claim, and win, the hand of Charlotte Herzog, a visitor from St. Louis, who with

Written 1985 and published in the *Contemporary Authors Autobiography Series*, vol. 4 (Detroit: Gale Research, 1986).

midwestern simplicity insisted on being called Lottie. Theirs was a classic American middle-class marriage, one in which the newly arrived male immigrant finds himself a genteel and acculturated wife from the previous generation of immigration, a wife whose father, upon immigration, had found himself a genteel and acculturated wife, *und so weiter.*

Lottie Herzog's father, Herman (a man determined enough to have deserted from both sides in the Civil War, the Union side first), had married Bella Cullman soon afterwards in Memphis, where, with his wife's brothers, he put in some good years in the tobacco business but did not choose to follow the Cullmans back to New York. (Too bad for him. Cullman Brothers later turned into Philip Morris.) Herman Herzog had to be content with respect, if not eminence, in wholesale dry goods in St. Louis. He hated the business cordially and turned it over to his son Fred in 1918. His wife too longed to join the Cullmans in New York, but did not do so until after Herman's death, in her old age. Their daughter Lottie, born in 1871, liked St. Louis well enough in the era of its World Fair. She taught German and French kindergarten there for a while. As a member of the St. Louis Ethical Culture Society she seems to have felt confident that she would seldom be stigmatized as a Jew. My own mother's decision, a generation later in 1926, to marry a gentile, a foreigner, a poet, and a bastard (for so my father in his pathetic moments chose to label himself) must have also risen out of some deep self-assurance that she and hers would not, could not, be rejected by America, that she was entitled to equity and prominence.

Youthful photographs of Natalie Weiner show a well-fed, lightly starched young woman, accustomed to a town house with maids. Her family lacked little in the material sense. Natalie was chauffeured from 375 West End Avenue to the Ethical Culture School on Central Park West, where she absorbed a moral imperative distinct from Judaism, tinged with a strong meliorative impulse, and developed a desire, owing little to any specific religious doctrine, to improve the condition of her fellows. She learned languages and played on a lovely Steinway A-model grand piano bought for the purpose in 1915, when she was sixteen. She was given a floor of her own in the Weiners' house furnished with the piano and with a new suite of walnut furniture, stained blue and upholstered in blue plush. The fall of 1917 saw her into Barnard College, where she made friends with bright girls whose marriages would scatter them across the country from Louisville to Milwaukee. When the World War and influenza epidemic were safely over, she traveled to Europe with her friend Marie Mayer, a thrilling journey described to us in after years with all the innocent flapper foolishness of *Our Hearts Were Young and Gay* by Cornelia Otis Skinner and Emily Kimbrough.

The socially conscious young woman found herself one job as a cub reporter on Walter Lippmann's New York *Daily World* and another with the New York State Department of Labor, whose Secretary, under Governor Al Smith, was the redoubtable Madam Frances Perkins. And she fell in love. Not suitably, not with one of the nice Columbia boys like Bennett Cerf or Dick Simon or Harold Guinzburg, who were thinking of founding publishing houses, but with a married man, the playwright Elmer Rice. The affair had nowhere to go. It stopped, and my mother had a collapse. Colitis was diagnosed. Psychotherapy (Jungian) was called for. After a few months my grandfather took my mother to Europe To Forget, and they embarked on a tour of family and friends in Vienna, Karlsbad, Trenčín, Rothenburg-ob-der-Tauber, and the cities of the Rhine. When my grandfather felt able to leave Natalie on her own, she went on to attend the Fabian Society Summer School in Sussex. Just before Christmas 1924, she met Edward Davison, employed at the time as the business manager of an Anglican Church weekly paper, *The Challenge,* in London.

Teddie Davison, like Natalie Weiner, stood at a crossroads. During his bright postwar career at Cambridge University he had been regarded by some as the successor to the poetic mantle of the martyred Rupert Brooke. In 1920, still an undergraduate, he had published his first volume of poems. In London, after graduation, he had shared quarters for a while with J. B. Priestley, critic, budding novelist, and playwright-to-be, who, like Teddie, had come up to Cambridge after five years in the war. Only my father's closest friends had been vouchsafed the truth: that Teddie was the illegitimate son of a gentlewoman named Evelyn Davison, who as governess to the Leeds family of a burgher named Edward Shields had been seduced in Edwardian fashion and then kept for years in a succession of modest lodgings in northern English cities. Though my father was born in Glasgow, on the fly, in 1898 (followed by his sister Amy in 1902), his mother did not marry Shields until 1917, after she read in the papers that the first Mrs. Shields was dead. It is odd to think that I must have a whole tribe of English cousins of my generation, two-and-a-half times removed, all unknown to me, as I am to them.

My father was sometimes in his infancy given over to the care of foster mothers, but for much of his childhood he grew up with his mother and his sister, and no father, in South Shields, 17 Porchester Street, Tyne Dock, in a four-room house without indoor plumbing or, of course, central heat. His soprano voice proved his salvation—his voice and the Church of England. He became a chorister, and he learned through the Church, that traditional educator of the poor, how to pronounce the English language "properly": how, by walking an acceptable tightrope of vowels, to take his place in the middle class beside his genteel mother. He left school at the age of twelve to find employment, now in an office, now in a factory, and finally as box-office manager of a music hall, but his voice—until it changed—brought him a little fame and a little money and confidence, singing solo anthems in South Shields and Newcastle and even as far afield as Durham Cathedral.

When the Great War broke out my father was sixteen. He lied about his age and volunteered for the Royal Navy. Once again his voice—now tenor—came to the rescue. Young men with proletarian accents who, like him, had enlisted in the Royal Naval Division, were shoveled into the ranks. My father's vowels won him an office job and a warrant-officer's commission, while his fellows spilled their blood to realize Winston Churchill's strategies on the beaches of Ostend and Gallipoli. For five-and-a-half years Teddie clerked in London at Royal Naval Division Headquarters in the Crystal Palace. In 1919 he qualified for a National Scholarship to St. John's College, Cambridge, despite his lack of secondary education. He was already publishing poems in the *London Mercury* and had fallen under the protectorship of its brilliant but unreliable editor, J. C. Squire. Squire promised to help my father through Cambridge, encouraged his expectations, and showed him by example what few have to be taught: to live beyond his means. By the time my mother arrived in London Teddie was already deeply in debt, and he had begun perhaps to suspect, in an age of poetry that was already beginning to tilt toward T. S. Eliot and Ezra Pound, that his moody lyrics and greensward ruminations might be edging out of fashion as well.

Edward Davison met Natalie Weiner at the house of their mutual friend Milton Waldman, an Anglo-American Jewish publisher and scholar, in December of 1924. Each had, I think, arrived with someone else, but they walked home through the dark streets together. My father sang. They enjoyed several weeks of intense courtship, and then my mother sailed for home. Teddie followed her the next summer, and they were married by Rabbi Stephen S. Wise in a hotel in New York on April 27, 1926, the last in the long family succession of marriages between the assimilated woman and the unassimilated man. Their wedding picture shows them sitting on a blue-walnut, plush-upholstered daybed, which eventually became my own and then my children's. This picture, when the time came, would serve on the jacket of my autobiography, for these two were already, as they sat there, setting the coordinates for my life.

After both my parents were dead I anatomized their marriage in a self-castigating memoir entitled *Half Remembered: A Personal History,* which began: "Home was the compartment of music and discord, the vessel of my mother's influence, the rostrum for my father's voice." I started out with dangerous diseases in early childhood, when life seemed to threaten rather than welcome me. My earliest memories are of Mill Pond House, a place my family rented from 1931 to 1933 near Peekskill, New York, on the side of a modest hill, where my father wrote poems and lectures in a shanty in a meadow and where he taught me to read. Indoors I often lay convalescing, but outdoors, beyond a ruined gristmill and above its milldam, lay a pond with a small boat house and decaying skiff. My early childhood was watchdogged by a Viennese nurse, worthy of a Freudian case study, whom my family had hired while abroad on a Guggenheim Fellowship, a *Kinderschwester* who seemed to me the personification of witchery. Though my happy memories of Mill Pond House call up sunlit meadows and reflections on the water, my more sinister recollections revolve around bedroom, bathroom, and kitchen, where Schwester slapped my *bupsch* and scolded my sister and me in vile Austrian. Fortunately Schwester soon left us, but not the memories of her tenure, which surfaced forty years later in the chiaroscuro of psychoanalysis, dominated by a vision of myself eyeless in Gaza, by the mill with slaves.

We moved again when I was five, closer to New York, into a large house that my grandparents helped my parents to buy, on Pinesbridge Road in Ossining, in nearly open country. The house is immense, as I recently confirmed after half a century—far larger even than my childhood memories of it. I recall a snowy winter with sleds; a vast vegetable garden planted in the spring by a hired man with a horse and harrow; chickens in the coop and ducks on the pond. I still lament the tragedy of a coveted gift, a green tricycle, which I carelessly left in the driveway, where the car backed over it and left it a twisted wreck before noon on Christmas Day.

After only a year in Ossining we moved on for a winter to Coral Gables, where my father, in the Great Depression of 1934–35, needed the official teaching job offered by the University of Miami to pad out the increasingly puny lecture engagements that were being offered. The spring of 1935 took us far across the dustblown Great Plains to Boulder, Colorado, which turned out, surprise, to be our hometown for a decade to come. Somehow we never made it back to the great house in Ossining. After several rentals in Boulder we settled, when I was ten, in a roomy granite house at 1313 University Avenue, near the edge of the University of Colorado campus. The house is the one I will always remember as home. The ground floor was where guests entered, where the piano sat and my parents made music and I practiced it, where the Latino maid, Beatrice Tafoya, cooked the meals. On the second floor, surrounding a trafficked central hallway, lay four bedrooms: one for my parents, one for my sister, one for the frequent houseguests, and one for me. On the third floor, yet another circle toward heaven, lay my father's study, where he wrote his lectures, entertained students at evening seminars, and, when the fit was upon him, spoke of composing poems. Alas, the fit grew increasingly rare, and even a child could sense that more attention went into the social festivities of Floor One than into the creative exercises of Floor Three.

Every summer for three weeks the house lay open during the Writers' Conference in the Rocky Mountains, which my parents directed every year between 1935 and 1942. During those red-letter weeks guests came and went at all hours—Robert Frost, Robert Penn Warren, Thomas Wolfe, Ford Madox Ford, Katherine Anne Porter, Elmer Rice, Ralph Hodgson, Carl Sandburg, Wallace Stegner, Paul Horgan, Robert Lowell, Jean Stafford, and dozens of other writers, old and young. Even in the winter months, visiting lecturers, performers, or artists would often occupy the guest room—the pianists Josef and Rosina Lhevinne, Harold Bauer, Percy Grainger, the mime Angna Enters, the painter Charles Hopkinson, the basso Alexander Kipnis, members of the Trapp Family Choir, and other celebrities who always emerged from somewhere to the east of us.

My father's third-floor library offered Melville, Scott, Cooper, Mark Twain, Dickens, Walter De la Mare, and a thousand others; and my father's omnipresent voice, quoting out of a fathomless memory lines from Shakespeare and Burns, Campion and Tennyson, Keats and Wordsworth and Robert Bridges, enriched the print of poetry with the thrilling dimensions of sound. My mother, who gave herself at this stage to the rearing of children, the entertainment of guests, the cultivation of flowers, and the study of piano, made the house a center of hospitality. In the afternoons it became a locus for committees of the League of Women Voters, the Association of University Women, and, later on, Finnish War Relief and Bundles for Britain.

My life outside the house was spacious, adventurous, competitive. I had put behind me all my childhood ailments. I studied clarinet and piano and German. I rode my bicycle everywhere in Boulder's hills and flatlands. I learned to hike in the mountains behind the Flatirons. I took up swimming and tennis and skating. I experienced the rigors of a climate starving for moisture by seeing to the watering of our own lawn and flowers. Colorado's air was clear and bright after the Dust Bowl years, as it is less often now that hydrocarbons have darkened it. As I grew older I ascended higher into the mountains on skis, and I was swiftly promoted in school. By twelve, I was ill-at-ease with my pubescent classmates of fourteen and fifteen, and the next year, none too soon, I was sent to Colorado Springs, to board at the Fountain Valley School, an Eastern oasis of learning, as it regarded itself, on the Western Plains.

It is no wonder, perhaps, that much of my writing is concerned with the implications of inheritance. A Jewish mother, something of an apostate, living in Colorado but loving New York. An Anglican father, who, having fled his homeland, yearned for its language and literature. A beloved younger sister, gay and uninhibited, whose laughter diverted itself into rhymes and song. A paradisal hometown from which I was banished to a boarding school where the boys (no girls) wore blue serge suits to dinner and white shirts with detachable collars and school ties. Home and school alike lay at the foot of wild dry mountains and depended on artificial irrigation for their survival. And, as though these contrasts did not concern us, at every opportunity my family trekked somewhere else, winter or summer, like ants whose nest had been kicked. I developed chronic car-sickness in the back seat of our blue Chevy on journeys between New York, Florida, Colorado, Arizona, Utah, Mississippi, Louisiana, California, New Mexico, and Wyoming, tires rattling over thousands of miles of prewar ribbed concrete two-laned highways. In 1943, when my father volunteered for his second tour of armed service—this time in the U.S. Army—we drove East again and ceased our family travels at last in Washington. My parents and sister spent the rest of the war there while I rode out my last two years of boarding school in Colorado Springs, traveling back and forth on the raucous day-coach trains of wartime.

The War, for boys like me, threatened the very idea of home and the prospect of a future. Our home had been abandoned, apparently for good. My classmates accelerated their schooling to make ready for the armed forces. I myself, on summer vacations in Washington, took civil service jobs: in 1944 as a page in the United States Senate, where I reported for work on the day the Allied Armies opened the Second Front in Normandy and spent the summer watching the capers of such statesmen as Henry A. Wallace, Robert A. Taft, Arthur Vandenberg, Alben Barkley, and Harry S. Truman. In 1945, as a supervisor on a public but still racially segregated playground, I heard on the radio President Truman announce the first news of Nagasaki. By this time I had graduated from the Fountain Valley School, too young for military service; I had developed competence in Latin, had picked up smatterings of French and German, had learned to act in plays and sing Gilbert and Sullivan, had heard the poetry of E. E. Cummings and T. S. Eliot and Archibald MacLeish read aloud by a redoubtable English teacher who was the husband of MacLeish's sister; had proved myself in track and basketball, had done some challenging and even dangerous mountain climbing, and had learned enough mathematics and science to fit me for the next stage of expectation.

But Harvard was not what I had expected: it was not what anyone had expected. Within ninety days after my matriculation in 1945 the buildings and classrooms filled to bursting with war veterans returned from the Murmansk Run, from New Caledonia, from the Apennines. Though my early friends at Harvard were teenagers like myself, still damp from Exeter or Middlesex or Belmont Hill, the second wave were much older men, veterans of the Burmese Highlands or B-24 raids over Europe, making ready to become writers or composers or publishers or college presidents. So far it had sufficed to observe and emulate the adult world, to listen to the conversation of my parents' authoritative older generation. These sinewy older Harvard men had been initiated in a way I could hardly emulate; but they accepted me as a friend nonetheless. The Radcliffe women were no older than I, as confused by the War's upheavals as I had been, and they were even further confused by the urgent demands of the grown men who wooed them.

Harvard after the war nearly at once burst out into the arts. The Veterans' Theatre Workshop, later to develop into the Brattle Theatre Repertory Company, presented Shakespeare and Shaw; the Harvard Glee Club, which lent its members to the Boston Symphony Orchestra for choral performances under Koussevitsky, Bernstein, Monteux, and others, enabled me to sing choral works by Beethoven, Brahms, Bach, Stravinsky, Mahler, Fauré, Palestrina, William Byrd. A tide of young poets (Kenneth Koch, John Ashbery, Robert Bly, Donald Hall, and, not yet known to me, L. E. Sissman) was flowing through Harvard, instructed by Theodore Morrison, Richard Wilbur, John Ciardi, and later Archibald MacLeish, but to me the writing of poetry was still a pursuit reserved for "adults." Like my father. Like Robert Frost.

Frost had long been a family friend. My mother had attended Barnard with Frost's daughter Lesley (who would lend her name to my sister Lesley and in turn to my daughter Lesley), and J. C. Squire, editor of the *London Mercury,* had given my father a letter to Frost when Teddie left London. While we lived in Coral Gables, Frost had come for a visit. Passing through Cambridge soon after I arrived at Harvard in 1945, my father took me to visit the old poet at home. I was immediately entranced with his way of talking, his irreverence for academic authority, his playful skepticism about the very education I was slavishly pursuing. Throughout my undergraduate years and later on, when I returned to Cambridge as an editor, Frost welcomed me to his house for an occasional afternoon or evening or would come to my house for a meal. He had a genius for friendship. I saw little—not nothing, but not much—of the jealous and self-serving careerist so vengefully portrayed by his biographer Lawrance Thompson, who somehow managed in his three-volume book not to convey the most vivid and obvious thing about the living Frost—his powerful physical presence. Frost's body could remain absolutely still in a chair for hours at a time, feet planted flat on the floor while he talked and paused and talked, his hands describing the gestures of weed-chopping or brushing away cobwebs, or other such motions from the world of work, while his voice turned the surges of his mind into play, something witty, rhythmic, exploratory. His talk was always in motion. Even when he repeated a story or idea you had heard before, he seemed to be chivvying it for something new.

Though my years at Harvard did much to make me "well educated," my studies did little to make me a poet. Abbott Lawrence Lowell is reputed to have burbled, "When we find a spark of talent at Harvard, we water it." But I must not blame Harvard overmuch. I was frightened of poetry, living poetry, perhaps because for years I had been watching my father lose touch with his gift. I listened to I. A. Richards lecture, with wizard brilliance, on the interactions between poetic statement and poetic meaning; I relished Walter Jackson Bate's passionate anatomization of the poetic techniques of Pope, Johnson, and Keats; I pored over the cadences of Matthew Arnold and Thomas Hardy and W. B. Yeats. I wandered through translations of Thucydides and Plato and Sophocles and Homer. But all the while I learned more about the nature of poetry by listening to the words of song while singing: the way poems and prayers took to the air gave me more vital understanding of the liveliness of the art than any college course did. Poetry didn't seem to me—in some ways it still does not—to be at home in college, and I have never, then or now, given or taken a course in the writing of poetry. Since my best friends were composers and musicians, I learned from them. When I finished Harvard in 1949 I knew more than I knew but less than I thought. As though my unconscious were telling me that the time had come for me to begin living, my handwriting had changed radically and no longer looked like that of a child.

I spent my first summer after graduation in Italy, much of it listening to harpsichord music in the master classes at Siena, where my Harvard friend Douglas Allanbrook, having studied composition with Nadia Boulanger, was now studying harpsichord with Ruggero Gerlin. Italy was just what my stifled emotions needed, and I went on, in October, to a year of residence thanks to the Fulbright program, at St. John's College, Cambridge University, with my senses awakened, a hundred experiences behind me and a thousand to absorb, and no longer, what a relief, a virgin! In the academic sense Cambridge proved as inhibiting as Harvard, though here mercifully the student was encouraged to take his education less from the faculty than with his fellow students. My luckiest friendships were with the fascinating Peter Shaffer, not yet writing plays but already showing signs of theatrical dedication, and the prodigious James Mossman, brooding over his study of history, who later became an excellent television journalist and possibly a spy but ended a suicide in 1971. We lunched, drank, dined, argued, walked and laughed. I have never laughed so hard as at Cambridge: the margins of my lecture notes are festooned with irreverent caricatures. But whatever other delights I found there, a new understanding of poetry was not among them.

Oh, how I longed to get away from schooling and into Life! I toyed with the thought of running away to London or Paris, but I had never yet lived in a metropolis for more than a few weeks, and I found the prospect daunting. In the Easter vacation of 1950 I ventured out in an old bicycle—carrying a Bible, as I did most of my year abroad—to pedal north along the west coast of Britain from Cornwall to the Lakes. It was my first extended venture into the open air since leaving Colorado five years before, and it reawakened a part of me that had slept restlessly indoors all this time. Along my way I composed a sequence of clerihews on the names of English towns and villages and sent them, with comically clumsy drawings, to my parents in New York (where they had settled at last) as a silver anniversary gift. Poetry, I began to realize, could very well come to me from the outdoors and from rural talk, the sort of talk I was listening to in pubs and marketplaces. I would not learn this lesson at once and would spend nearly a decade making good the loss of a sense of place, of identity with landscape, that I had left behind me on leaving the plains and mountains of Colorado.

In August, 1950, after a second European summer spent in Paris and Bavaria—a summer darkened by the arrival of the

Korean war—I said my goodbyes to my father's friends and relations in England (his sister Amy and his friend J. B. Priestley had been particularly generous) and, lifted on my way by an exultant and joyously impassioned love affair in London, returned to New York, where I had got an appointment as first reader at the distinguished publishing house of Harcourt, Brace. Along with Scribner's, Harper's, and Macmillan's, it was one of the last WASP publishing houses, now suffering increasingly stiff competition from the newer houses (Randon House, Simon and Schuster, and the Viking Press) mostly founded in the 1920s by my mother's Columbia friends. Harcourt in 1950 was at the height of its publishing distinction, already known as the publisher of all the Bloomsbury eminences—Keynes, Forster, the Woolfs, Strachey, et al.—as well as the most distinguished list of female fiction writers in America, among them Katherine Anne Porter, Eudora Welty, Jean Stafford, Mary McCarthy, and Flannery O'Connor; as well as many poets and pillars of litcrit: T. S. Eliot, Robert Penn Warren, John Crowe Ransom, I. A. Richards, Cleanth Brooks, R. P. Blackmur, William Empson, Carl Sandburg, Robert Lowell, Richard Wilbur, and Randall Jarrell.

I would spend the next five years at Harcourt, Brace, less two years of service in the Army at locations in Massachusetts, Kansas, Texas, and North Carolina. My military assignment, most of the time, was as a noncommissioned officer in the Second Loudspeaker and Leaflet Company, training for "psychological warfare" against an undetermined foe. I was discharged in March, 1953, the day after the death of Josef Stalin.

I have always looked back at two pleasures in my Army experience: the actual basic military training, which, rigorous as it was, mostly took place in the open air; and the rich variety of American speech I encountered from all over the nation among cooks, ministers, professors, truck drivers, printers, refugees, urban blacks, bar girls, rural blacks, fellow-choristers, and all the mad variety of a peacetime war. In addition, while in Kansas among the clement limestone hills around Fort Riley, I finally confronted the actualities of religious faith. All the years in which my mother had dodged religious issues, all my years of singing in choirs and hearing the incantatory resonances of the Church of England now took me, one October weekend, by surprise. I felt, quite literally, as though God had spoken to me.

> But as I rav'd and grew more fierce and wilde
>> At every word,
> Me thought I heard one calling, *Childe:*
> And I reply'd, *My Lord.*

The paternal English side of my ancestry now stated its most powerful claim through the language of the King James Bible. Because of the glimmering language I could never acknowledge with equal allegiance my Jewish side, even though by Jewish law I will always be regarded as a Jew. To be Jewish is not a matter of choice but of destiny; to be Christian is to consent and embrace a faith. To the bemusement of the religious of both creeds, I believe I belong to both; but when I am honest with myself I have to acknowledge the truth that, for the sake of language, I cannot limit myself to the Old Testament. I guess I would rather be a bad Christian than a bad Jew. For several years after my Kansas baptism and confirmation I remained conscientious in my churchly kneeling and singing; but the attitudes of prayer eventually found their way permanently into my poetry, and particularly into the title (*Praying Wrong*) of my 1984 volume of selected poems.

After my discharge and return to New York and Harcourt, Brace in 1953, I spent two years losing my pleasure in both the city and the Company. My father became president of the Poetry Society of America (though he no longer wrote any) and dean of general studies of Hunter College (though he no longer taught); my mother became professionally active in Americans for Democratic Action and in New York Democratic reform politics. I settled in with a series of roommates, beginning with my sister, in a charming apartment in a Murray Hill brownstone, but my two principal activities were both voracious: learning about publishing and chasing girls. Overdoses threatened in both departments. In early 1955 Harcourt, Brace's management changed dramatically when William Jovanovich, a tall, imperious man whom I remembered as a University of Colorado student in the late 1930s, became president of the company. His management caused the resignation of most of the editors and the departure of many of the authors whose presence had validated the work I did there; and a lucky recommendation from Eugene Reynal soon enabled me to move back to Massachusetts, as assistant to the revered Thomas J. Wilson, director of Harvard University Press, a man whom I came to like enormously. I was not sorry to put some distance between me and my family, nor to abandon the metropolis, nor to say goodbye to the woman with whom I had formed my first extended love-relationship, nor even to part with my few New York friends outside publishing circles. New York was not the place for me: at twenty-seven— the same age at which my father had left England—I had found a profession and had decided where to live, but I had not decided how. The years 1955 and 1956 began to cancel such postponements.

My new job at Harvard was interesting but not very difficult. I had a little apartment all to myself. In the search for new female companionship I telephoned Sylvia Plath, newly graduated from Smith, where I had met her the previous spring on the recommendation of Alfred Kazin, her teacher. Sylvia was summering in Wellesley and preparing to go to Cambridge University in the fall. There was a lot she wanted to know about publishing; but as it turned out she taught me more about poetry than I could teach her about the book trade. Sylvia was already devoured by literary ambition and was assiduously in training to achieve it. She had written dozens of poems, many of which fill the juvenilia of her *Collected Poems,* and I read, or heard her read, many of those sedulous villanelles and acrobatic caprices. I was far less impressed by the poems she was actually writing than by the furious intensity of her preparation. She had studied contemporary poetry like coastal charts before a voyage, and she enthused about makers I had never heard about—Isabella Gardner, George Barker, Theodore Roethke. She played me her Dylan Thomas records, and we swooned together like teenagers. She also had a tale of her own to tell, the story of breakdown and attempted suicide and recovery that can be read in *The Bell Jar*. The version I heard in 1955, only two years after the actual event, was a tenderer, less sardonic narrative than the novel presents. Whatever the meaning of this confession, she soon seemed to regret having made it. After a dinner at her mother's house, only a month after the beginning of our affair, she took me for a walk and spoke in such a way as to retract such affection as had infused our lovemaking. She was on the lookout for a man whose strength and gifts would anchor her instability, and I was at best, as she must have known, a leaky life preserver. After arriving in England she would find those qualities in Ted Hughes, who—no matter how things ended after their marriage—understood her gift and her nature better than anyone else has.

Soon after Sylvia left Boston, I gravitated to the Poets' Theatre in Cambridge and auditioned for their production of Molière's *The Misanthrope*. In this great play, in Richard Wilbur's first verse translation, I played the part of Alceste, at once the most notable and the most ridiculous of heroes. I spent most of the autumn rehearsing and performing this role and learning my way around in Wilbur's shimmering and supple verse. An actor reimagines his lines onstage every night, and I could not have devised a more thorough training in verse technique. My father, after a trip to Boston to watch, wrote me to say that I was a good actor, but he thought I could become a better writer. It was the blessing of Isaac upon Jacob. A prohibition had been lifted, and a frightening challenge delivered.

It was now December, 1955. This crowded year had left me crestfallen and dejected, so deeply that I sought help in psychoanalysis—for the first time, but not, alas, for the last. Over the next three years the care of M. Robert Gardner would gradually free me from the compulsions of my erotic trifling, open my eyes to the nature of wholehearted love, and enable me to start writing poetry at last. As advertised, psychoanalysis taught me how to love and how to work.

In late 1956 I yielded to the repeated invitations of Seymour Lawrence, an old friend and onetime poet, to join his staff at the Atlantic Monthly Press. I would remain at work there, serving both the book publishing arm and its body, *The Atlantic Monthly,* for the next twenty-nine years, and I am still connected to *The Atlantic* today. I also fell in love with Nell Halsted, granddaughter of my family's friend Charles Hopkinson the painter, and I often visited their beautiful family estate on the North Shore in Manchester-by-the-Sea. By late 1957, and I do not attribute it to choice, I began to write poems, the precise circumstances of which I have described elsewhere in this book, on pages 113 and 178. It seems I had to become part of New England, part of its very landscape, in order to write poetry at all. The desire had walked unenacted with me in the Colorado mountains, had ridden with me along the roads of Devonshire and Gloucestershire, had lain with me on Army bivouacs and maneuvers in Kansas and Texas. Like so many other Americans, I found myself as a writer living off a land to the east of my psychic origins.

The *Atlantic* celebrated its centennial in 1957. The elegant and magisterial Edward Weeks, at fifty-nine, was at the peak of his career as editor; Seymour Lawrence, only thirty, was building his reputation as a fiction publisher while directing the Atlantic Monthly Press, and Arthur H. Thornhill the elder was steering Little, Brown and its Atlantic copublisher to prosperity. Boston, moreover, was about to become, for a few years, a peerless arena for poetry. Nowhere else in America were so many good poets working. A mere handful of those who were resident in the late fifties includes Robert Frost, Archibald MacLeish, Adrienne Rich, Robert Lowell, Sylvia Plath and Ted Hughes (newly but temporarily returned from England), Maxine Kumin, Anne Sexton, Richard Wilbur, Philip Booth, Stanley Kunitz, R. V. Cunningham, and George Starbuck. V. R. Lang and the Poets' Theatre were staging dramatic productions by John Ashbery, Kenneth Koch, W. S. Merwin, James Merrill, and poetry readings by dozens of others. Harvard, under the benign curatorship of John L. Sweeney, paid more attention to new American poetry than it had in a century. Charles Olson and his coterie were coalescing in Gloucester. It was not the worst time and place for a poet-come-lately.

My poetry grew, in my own eyes at least, beyond apprenticeship exercises and became a hot necessity of life after my relationship with Nell died out in 1958 and she married another man. I mourned, loonlike, for months, writing my way into my work via the back door of grief—an all-too familiar route. I showed some early pieces to Ted Hughes and Sylvia, who gave generous advice, and to Robert Frost, who said little but asked to see more. May Sarton spoke encouragingly of my early poems, John L. Sweeney invited me to record them for the Harvard Library, and colleagues at the *Atlantic* were positively and perennially supportive. Edward Weeks asked me to write annual reviews of other people's new poetry, and he printed many of my own. But the lion's share of my time was spent editing books for the Atlantic Monthly Press for publication under the Atlantic-Little, Brown imprint.

In 1958 I learned that my mother, in New York, had cancer; and on a visit to see her several months later, I met Jane Truslow, whom I knew within hours I wanted to marry. As Joan Didion wrote me about Jane many years later, "I met her when [we were] twenty . . . and she was the smartest and most sensible and funniest and kindest and generally the most enchanting girl I had ever met. She seemed to have exactly the right angle on everything and everyone . . . and she suggested by her example that everything could be all right. . . . This sense I had of her never changed." Jane had a way of transforming the mundane into the witty with a conniving sparkle of her blue eyes, a rueful grimace, a wave-it-off wisecrack. She was instantly adorable, and, as much for her diffidence as for her charm, promptly adored. My Boston friends fell for her the moment I brought her up from New York. My parents were delighted. I was grateful as a puppy that I had finally, at thirty, found the only woman I had ever unhesitatingly wanted.

Jane and I were married within weeks of our meeting. She left her job in New York publishing and took another in Cambridge as assistant editor of the John Harvard Library reprint series of Harvard University Press under my beloved professor Howard Mumford Jones, who lent us his Vermont farmhouse for our honeymoon. Soon after our marriage, in the summer of 1959, my mother relapsed and died, slowly, painfully, and horribly of cancer, which metastasized from kidney to spine to brain and left her suffering, speechless, and mercifully, at long last, lifeless a day beyond her sixtieth birthday. I wrote a suite of elegies, "Not Forgotten," before and after the actual event. Like so many elegies, they said more about the poet's grief than about the loved one.

The focus of my emotional life had already shifted easily to Jane, while the pattern of my days settled increasingly into the calendars of the publishing trade. I continued writing poetry, nearly all of which, somewhere in its cadences, was meant for Jane's ears, but though my daily work became more assiduous and administrative, I began gathering a clan of authors: Farley Mowat the Canadian, Dan Jacobson the South African, Harry M. Caudill the Kentuckian, and Robert Coles, the Massachusetts child psychiatrist who was already at work on the beginnings of his "Children of Crisis" series. I got interested in books on architecture (*The Architecture of America* by John Burchard and Albert Bush-Brown), psychology (I persuaded C. G. Jung to make a little book of an *Atlantic* essay, and *The Undiscovered Self* is still in print after nearly thirty years), anthropology, politics, history, and biography; but the larger portion of my time was spent in managing the schedules of books for other editors until, in 1964, Seymour Lawrence ceased to be director of the Atlantic Monthly Press, and Edward Weeks asked me to take over.

By this time Jane and I had two children: Angus, born in 1960, and Lesley, born in 1963. Thanks to an inheritance from my grandmother, we owned a red clapboard house on an unfashionable Cambridge side street. Our friends were mostly professional Cambridge types—attorneys, publishers, writers, psychiatrists, scholars. I continued my poetry reviews for *The Atlantic* and elsewhere, and I wrote music reviews, mostly of choral concerts, for the weekly Boston *Jewish Advocate*. More centrally, however, poems had bloomed out of my marriage. In April, 1961, just as the United States was attempting to invade the Bay of Pigs, I drove with George Starbuck and Anne Sexton to a literary festival at Cornell, where I gave my first poetry reading with Anne. In 1963 I completed my first book, *The Breaking of the Day,* which to my delight Dudley Fitts chose to win the Yale Series of Younger Poets Competition.

This success came at a strange juncture—hard after the deaths, two weeks apart, of Robert Frost and Sylvia Plath, neither of whom would ever see my first book. My last contact with each poet had been in December, 1962. Sylvia had sent me, from England, a large group of her intense late poems, including the daunting "Purdah," "The Jailer," and her sequence of beekeeping poems, two of which I'd eagerly persuaded Ted Weeks to accept for *The Atlantic.* These were published in April, 1963, shortly after the shock of her death in February. Jane and I stared at one another after reading *The Bell Jar* later in the spring. Both Jane and Sylvia had lost their fathers and had been sent to Smith College by widowed mothers (both of whom outlived their daughters). Both lived in a scholarship dormitory called Lawrence House, both majored in English, both had studied with Alfred Kazin. Both had been Guest Editors at *Mademoiselle.* Both, too, had broken down under psychic strain, and both recovered to graduate with high honors in 1955. Sylvia in a way belonged to us both, and when Jane turned to writing, in *The Fall of a Doll's House: Three Generations of American Women and the Houses They Lived In* (1980) she would write about their common inheritance, as I would write about Sylvia in *Half Remembered* and in poems like "The Heroine."

Jane and I had seen Frost just before his last hospitalization, when he stayed up half the night at our house quizzing Alastair Reid about his Scottish childhood. I had already asked Frost whether I might dedicate my first book to him. In the event, a year after his death, he shared the dedication of *The Breaking of the Day* with my father.

One could infer, from the posthumous careers of these two poets, how deeply poets could be misunderstood. Frost, the more tempered, accepted the omen during his lifetime when he growled to me one night, "I want people to understand me; I want them to understand me wrong." Sylvia, hesitating as she did between ladies' magazine fiction and the volcanoes of poetry while struggling to attain her generation's notions of perfection as wife and mother, threw herself at last into the crater, but first she wrestled openly, attempting to remake herself in her poetry. Both poets had, as young people, sacrificed more than most others do to alter their way of understanding themselves, and both would be, as Keats had written, "among the English poets at my death." Sylvia could never have guessed at the way in which her concluding gesture might be vulgarized for propaganda purposes, just as Frost could not have guessed how his chosen biographer would distort the tone and tenor of his life. As Keats also wrote, "That which is creative must create itself." Poetry is a gift, not a role. "Admit," I would write later on in reflecting on another suicide, John Berryman's, "that poetry is one of the dangerous trades." Anyone—Plath, Frost, Berryman—who writes in such a way as to epitomize the self must anticipate the confusion that readers will make between what one *is* and what one has *made*. If we write, and we often do, in an effort to keep ourselves sane, neither reader nor writer can be certain what is fact, what is fancy. We are divided; we are not divided.

I worked each year in the 1960s a little harder at publishing, and it became each year a little harder to squeeze out the time for poems. On weekends I would walk with friends and watch birds, which know how to fly away from danger. The poems, also like birds, in their mysterious way kept arriving, and so did my early collections embodying inner division— *The City and the Island* in 1966 and *Pretending to Be Asleep* in 1970, both published by Atheneum. But my props began to creak after 1968, a year in which a whole series of deaths at *The Atlantic* and in my family and among older friends (to say nothing of Martin Luther King, Jr., and Robert Kennedy) began to undermine the convictions of youth and bring on, as I passed forty, the anxieties of middle age. Finally, in early 1970, my father died of cirrhosis of the liver and, only two weeks after him, Arthur H. Thornhill of Little, Brown, a beloved protector of mine, succumbed to a heart attack. I spent my free time in the summer of 1970 sorting my father's papers and writing an elegy, "Dark Houses," an inverse biography in verse of my father's poetic career.

I was more than tired, I was in danger. I needed to get away from New England for a while. Jane agreed to the adventure and persuaded the children it would be exciting. Garth Hite, *The Atlantic*'s new publisher (who had, as it happens, been my father's student at Colorado) and Robert Manning, the editor, agreed to my request for leave without pay. We decided to spend a year in Rome beginning in the autumn of 1971. I applied for a Guggenheim Fellowship and was refused. We lived on savings, on a most welcome award from the National Institute of Arts and Letters, and on the money from a small coincidental inheritance, and the Rockefeller Foundation took me in for a month at the Villa Serbelloni at Bellagio. Jane began to explore the history of architecture, which after our return to Boston she would take up professionally. And I found Rome—to the surprise of many—an ideal place to work. The net result was *Half Remembered: A Personal History,* published by Harper and Row in 1973, and the following year in England, where it appeared simultaneously with my fourth book of poems, *Walking the Boundaries,* the book in which I think I hit my stride as a poet and began, as one well might in one's forties, to gather together the strands of my life.

On my return from Italy in 1972 I had accepted, in addition to my book publishing work, the job of choosing the poems for *The Atlantic* as its poetry editor, a job I have held ever since. As director of the Atlantic Monthly Press I carried administrative responsibilities that had increased since Rome. Yet I knew that, whatever else happened, a part of me was dedicated to my farm in West Gloucester. When my mother's uncle Fred Herzog, the last of my St. Louis family, died in 1968, he left me enough to buy a yellow Greek Revival cottage and some beautiful acreage by a salt marsh a mile from the sea. My father's ashes had, at his earnest plea, been scattered there after his death, as my stepmother's would be after hers. While I worked in Italy dreams of Gloucester had kept visiting me and instigating a new kind of poem. The aspect of my imagination that surrendered only to outdoor air ("The Two of You," "The Woodcock") had taken Gloucester as its soul's country. Increasingly, back in America, I found Gloucester and its craggy coastal landscape pushing in as foreground or background for my poems. I wrote a series of longish pieces,

"Walking the Boundaries," as a tour of my property's seasons and edges. My poems began fastening on a tree, a rock, a field, a tidal creek, a bird, and endowing these "natural things" with sacramental importance. *I shall not take / My bodily shape from any natural thing*, indeed!

In 1974 I pressed this trend farther when writing a centenary paper about Robert Frost for delivery at the Library of Congress, trying to imagine how Frost, coming out of the West, invented New England for himself in 1911–12. In 1975, further exploring the life of things, I began farming in a small way, keeping pigs, then sheep, with the partnership of a neighbor. Something had altered permanently as a consequence of my sojourn in the Eternal City, a unification of sensibility that took my work beyond the agonies of "encounter and struggle," as Dudley Fitts had characterized my first book. From *Dark Houses*, written in 1970, for the next decade and a half, nearly all my poetry would take its beginning or end from Gloucester's sparse and stony landscape. The migration of my sensibility had been fulfilled. After a 1974 business trip to London I found myself composing poems of farewell to England. I also managed to return to Colorado nearly every year in the 1970s, and each of these visits brought me back again to childhood touchstones, as in "Creatures of the Genitive" and "Atmospheres." Though it would be out of place to detail them here, my publishing decisions, like my writing, took on a bit more depth. I seem to have learned to take some confidence in my judgment, enabling me to predict, if not what the masses, at least what educated readers, might value.

Jane moved, in the 1970s, toward a new phase of her own. As our children grew up and prepared to leave home, she began preparing herself to launch out, at long last, into writing. In 1973 she edited a successful cookbook. In 1974, as an experiment, we wrote one piece jointly for the *New York Times Magazine*, and such assignments proliferated for her into an impressive series on renovated architecture. By 1977 we had moved out of our house in Cambridge (our friends, entrenched there, thought us so brave!) into a mixed-income housing project on the new Boston waterfront. I published *A Voice in the Mountain* at about this time, and I also edited *Hello*,

*Darkness,* the collected poems of my friend L. E. Sissman, who had died in 1976. Jane began a book about the lives and homes of three generations of American housewives, which she would entitle *The Fall of a Doll's House* (1980), sharing its title with one of my poems. Jane's book, however, would also encompass an aspect of our lives together that I never had the insight to describe, the ways in which men depend on women and women accept the weight of the dependence. John Updike, who knows about such issues, described it as "a polemic of rare good humor."

After two years on the waterfront Jane finished her book, and in a reassessment of our lives we decided not to look back to Cambridge. Both of our children, now in their teens, had finished school there. The town we had once loved, the 1950s college town, had in two decades taken on a glossy operational affluence that comprised all the distorted ambitions of the Kennedy and Nixon years. America had changed, and so had we: it was with a sense of renewal that we sold our Cambridge house to Lesley College and determined to move to the country full time in June, 1979.

Our next two years would be both our most intimate and our most harrowing. In the same week we moved to Gloucester Jane found a lump in her breast. She had, as it turned out, just two years to live. She rented a pied-à-terre on Commonwealth Avenue, where she could work during the day, and most evenings we would board the commuter train from Boston to Gloucester together. She continued working through the months of chemotherapy and of remission, writing a second book, *This Old House,* based on a popular public television show. It was published in 1980, only a few months after her first book. In the years since, *This Old House,* whose authors are listed as Bob Vila and Jane Davison, has sold ten times more copies than all of my own books taken together. In 1980 I published an anthology of selections, with preface, from the works of an old friend and Atlantic Monthly Press author entitled *The World of Farley Mowat.*

My life and my work cannot be separated from Jane's during these last years. In late 1979, after four years of earnest entreaty from me, the Atlantic Monthly Press allowed me to relinquish its directorship, which passed to my longtime associate Upton Birnie Brady, and this allowed me to concentrate my editorial responsibilities on my authors rather than on managing a publishing list. I was also writing the poems of country matters published in 1981 as *Barn Fever and Other Poems;* I would soon write the anxious sequence called "Wordless Winter," and I was doing what I could to nurse Jane through the cycle of her illness. In the fall of 1980, just before its darkest phase, we were able to travel together to Sicily and Umbria, to visit our friends Shirley and Francois Caracciolo in Todi and to return to Gloucester for the last act. Jane set up a screened tent in the meadow to ward the sun off her chemotherapy-sensitized skin, and in that beautiful place she sat out the lengthening days of spring, receiving farewell visits from friends, setting her house in order, and watching the unchanging rocks and changing woods of Gloucester till she slipped away on July 4, 1981, just fifty-three years after the day I first came home from the hospital to my first home in New York. She was forty-nine.

James Dickey, reviewing my *Praying Wrong*, in 1984, wrote, "Davison himself is a man with a great capacity for loving and a terrible apprehension over losing it, over the loss or straying of the beloved." For a while in 1981 it seemed to me as though I might lose everyone and everything. My daughter Lesley had just graduated from boarding school and had settled on college in California, distancing herself, no doubt, from the sorrows of home. My son Angus had already settled into his working life in Belmont, Massachusetts, and seemed bound for engagement and marriage, which happily ensued, as did, eventually, two grandchildren. Jane's mother, one of the dearest of women, showed us another example of survival and dedication. I had to make a new life. I was reeling with grief.

As Jane's illness had worsened, and even before, I had yet again sought the challenges and consolations of psychoanalysis, this time with a gifted and kindly young Finnish doctor named Gunilla Enlund Jainchill, who knew and admired Jane. She helped me through the deepest convulsions of mourning and the new course thereafter. I found help from men and women friends alike. In Gloucester, where the children and I buried Jane's ashes not far from all the others, and where, obedient to her instructions, I had conducted her memorial service, I found myself posing like Orpheus with his lyre, making the trees to move. It could easily have turned into too luxurious a grief. To counter that temptation I threw myself into extra work, fund-raising for Yaddo in New York, serving the National Endowment for the Arts in Washington. I traveled wherever possible—to Nova Scotia to visit Farley and Claire Mowat; to Texas, Utah, and California for poetry readings; to Japan and Hawaii out of curiosity; to Italy again and, more happily, to Portugal and Spain, where Lesley spent her junior year of college.

Eight months after Jane's death I began spending time with Joan Goody, a beautiful and gifted architect, whose husband and partner Marvin Goody had died a year before Jane. The two women had met once; Jane had admired Joan's housing designed for the elderly; Joan came to admire Jane's books; I came to love what Marvin had done for Joan. Time, as we warily sized one another up, brought Joan and me gradually, then more swiftly, together. At length we decided to join our lives, and Joan redesigned my house in Gloucester and her own house in Boston not only to accommodate herself and me, but to lay some of our ghosts. We would divide our time between the two places.

On August 11, 1984, Joan and I were married in Cambridge, in Agassiz House, a beautiful theater building Joan had recently renovated for Radcliffe College where I, thirty-six years before, had acted a role in George Bernard Shaw's *Getting Married*. My sister Lesley, her husband Forrest Perrin, and their children Wendy and Scott, made the music for us; friends made speeches; I recited poems and sang "Drink to Me Only with Thine Eyes." Several months later I published *Praying Wrong: New and Selected Poems, 1957–1984* with a last dedication to Jane, beloved companion of nearly all those years. In the poems that have come to me since my second marriage I detect a different sort of dedication, a haunting by time, a deeper engagement with the future of the earth. (These poems were published in *The Great Ledge* in 1989.)

At the end of 1985 the time came for me to sever my

connection with the Atlantic Monthly Press after twenty-nine years and to strike out on my own as an editor before the press was sold to new owners and moved to New York. I would happily continue to choose the poetry for *The Atlantic*, whose ownership and direction did not change, but now I would begin editing "Peter Davison Books" for Houghton Mifflin Company, the alert yet venerable publishing house that had long stood directly across the Boston Common from *The Atlantic*, and that had even, for much of the nineteenth century, owned the magazine. But from now on, after a career of allegiance to institutions, I would be working for myself and would, I imagined, move toward the pleasure of old age responsible to no one but myself, my wife, my terrain, my children and grandchildren, and my poetry. "Best ask for gifts," as I had written twenty years earlier, "as though I had none coming."

## UNDER DISCUSSION
### Donald Hall, General Editor

Volumes in the Under Discussion series collect reviews and essays about individual poets. The series is concerned with contemporary American and English poets about whom the consensus has not yet been formed and the final vote has not been taken. Titles in the series include:

**Elizabeth Bishop and Her Art**
*edited by Lloyd Schwartz and Sybil P. Estess*
**Richard Wilbur's Creation**
*edited and with an Introduction by Wendy Salinger*
**Reading Adrienne Rich**
*edited by Jane Roberta Cooper*
**On the Poetry of Allen Ginsberg**
*edited by Lewis Hyde*
**Robert Bly: When Sleepers Awake**
*edited by Joyce Peseroff*
**Robert Creeley's Life and Work**
*edited by John Wilson*
**On the Poetry of Galway Kinnell**
*edited by Howard Nelson*
**On Louis Simpson**
*edited by Hank Lazer*
**Anne Sexton**
*edited by Steven E. Colburn*
**James Wright**
*edited by Peter Stitt and Frank Graziano*
**Frank O'Hara**
*edited by Jim Elledge*
**On the Poetry of Philip Levine**
*edited by Christopher Buckley*

Forthcoming volumes will examine the work of Langston Hughes, Muriel Rukeyser, H.D., and Denise Levertov, among others.

*Please write for further information on available editions and current prices.*

*Ann Arbor*          **The University of Michigan Press**